Decoding Dyslexia

Decoding Dyslexia

14 programmes for helping dyslexia
& the active ingredient
they share

Jennifer Poole PhD

Matador
9 De Montfort Mews
Leicester LE1 7FW, UK
Tel: (+44) 116 255 9311 / 9312
Email: books@troubador.co.uk
Web: www.troubador.co.uk/matador

ISBN 978-1906510-510

Typeset in 12pt Times New Roman by Troubador Publishing Ltd, Leicester, UK
Printed by The Cromwell Press Ltd, Trowbridge, Wilts, UK

Matador is an imprint of Troubador Publishing Ltd

CONTENTS

ACKNOWLEDGMENTS

I would like to thank Prof. Bob Burden for his open-minded generosity. Without him this research would never have taken place. And also my partner, Mike Franklin, without whom it would never have been published.

This work is an overview of the current field and draws on every specialist branch in an attempt to link them into a unified theory. Consequently, it is an enhancement of the work currently being undertaken by many, many, other people. I would particularly like to thank all those who so kindly answered my questions over the seven years of the PhD research which formed *Decoding Dyslexia*: in particular Phil Bayliss, Alan Costall, Rod Nicolson, Ute Frith and Margaret Snowling.
Thank you all.

Illustration Credit
The Causal Model of Dyslexia by Ute Frith (figure 2, Chapter 1) is taken from: *Dyslexia* (2nd Edition) by Margaret Snowling (2000) and appears by permission of Blackwell Publishing.

A child's representation of 'Over' in clay (Figure 8, chapter 5) is published with thanks to Hilary Farmer.

LIST OF TABLES AND FIGURES

Tables

Figures

INTRODUCTION

If you are familiar in any way with the subject of dyslexia you may have heard teachers or politicians talking about 'phonics programmes' or of using 'a multisensory approach'. If you have a child with dyslexia you might have been offered one of these programmes in school. You may even know what these expressions mean.

Or, perhaps like me prior to this study, you are completely unfamiliar and have no clear idea. As a psychology student I became fascinated with how children develop handedness and the difference this makes in other areas of their development, so I chose to study dyslexia in order to gain more understanding of how the brain wired itself for different purposes. I had no experience of dyslexia myself, and no prior knowledge of the mass of research into literacy and brain functioning. No one I knew taught dyslexic children and no family members had reading problems. I was soon astonished at how diverse the many programmes for helping children with dyslexia are. There is no single programme offered in all schools and some have nothing to do with literacy at all. Interestingly, according to the children and parents who used them, they all seemed to work – at least for some children. This intriguing fact formed the essence of this study in which I attempted to discover what such diverse programmes might have in common and what this could tell us about dyslexia itself. Chapter 1 describes the current approach of programmes for dyslexia and the theories which underpin them. Chapters 2–7 describe the theory and practice of the 14 different programmes in the study and Chapter 8 how they were analysed. In Chapter 9, *Orientation Theory* is explored in the context of child development. Finally, Chapter 10 gives practical advice drawn from the study findings on how to bring about orientation in both literacy and pre-school years.

CHAPTER 1

INTERVENTION PROGRAMMES IN DYSLEXIA

There are a great many different interventions for children with dyslexia, which generally fall within three streams. These are phonological, multisensory, and non-literary approaches. Those available in schools (and privately outside of it) are reading-based but there are many which do not directly focus on literacy. These range from nutritional supplementation and exercise programmes to making music. This chapter will outline the rationale behind the three major approaches and the different theories behind them, before turning in the next chapter to the 14 chosen to be part of the study undertaken to answer the question: "How can such different programmes all be helpful – especially those with nothing to do with reading?"

Phonological Programmes

Words are made up of small sounds, called phonemes, which are put together to form syllables and then whole words, as shown in Fig 1 on page 4.

Reading is a system of paired-associate learning, where the visual written code (graphemes) or *orthography* must be learned with its representational spoken sounds (phonemes). Children usually become

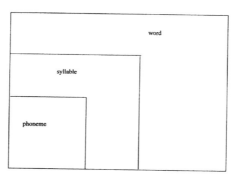

Fig.1 The make-up of words

able to break down words into their syllables at about 4 years of age, but phoneme-recognition does not emerge until later at about 5-6 years.

At present, the most popular theory of dyslexia is that it represents a problem in processing phonemes. This 'phonological weakness' is generally accepted to be the 'core deficit' in the specific learning problem of dyslexia. A carefully structured phonetic-based scheme will initially avoid whole words and teach sounds (phonemes) first, working up to chunks of words (syllables) and continually revising what has been learned. Phonic skills alone, however, are not sufficient in reading as they provide only the basis for recognising sounds in words. Other factors such as fluency are also important. The *Sheffield Programme*, a 10-hour phonics and fluency remediation, for example, designed by Nicolson and Fawcett, has been compared with simpler phonics programmes and found to be generally more effective. So, although phonological skills are now fully emphasised in the National Curriculum the manner in which phonemes are taught to children with dyslexia tends to vary with some proponents emphasising fluency, analogy, analysis and/or synthesis in addition to phonemes, (Fawcett, 2002). Consequently a great many different programmes for teaching children with dyslexia exist. In essence phonological programmes vary only in the 'mix' and emphasis they place on the skills of learning the associations of sounds with the code of language. Each programme emphasises learning to use phonemes, but each utilises different methods for learning to associate them with graphemes, the written signs of language.

The Theory Behind Phonological Programmes

Many theorists believe that dyslexia has a genetic origin, which is why it runs in families. A large-scale study of twins appears to support this. (TEDS 2006). The suggestion is that faulty genes bring about changes from usual brain function resulting on the 'behavioural' level in the literacy problems of dyslexia, plus any other impairments specific to that child, as in Fig 2 below.

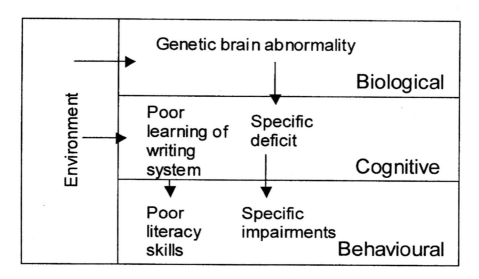

Fig.2 Frith's causal modelling diagram applied to dyslexia.
From: Snowling, (2000), p27

However, at present there has been no 'gene for dyslexia' found although several different genes have been highlighted. For example, phonological problems have been strongly associated with Chromosome 6 (Cardon et.al, 1994; Grigorenko et. al, 1997). There is a weaker link to Chromosome 15 for single-word reading (Grigorenko et.al, 1997) while 36 members of a family of 80 established a relevant genetic association with Chromosome 2 (Fagerheim et al, 1999). This has led to the proposal that several genes interact with factors in the environment to bring about the changes in the brain, which underlie dyslexia. Estimates range from 25-50% gene involvement (Blakemore & Frith, 2005; Olson, 2004). In other words the individual may have a 50% 'risk' of dyslexia (which may or may not run in their family) but without the environmental factor(s) this would not in itself be sufficient to result in dyslexia.

In Fig 2 above, the environmental factor suggested is the English orthography, which is known to be difficult and frequently illogical. It is much easier, for example, to learn to read Italian. So the 50% 'risk' might not be triggered if a different orthography were taught to the 'at risk' child. Other environmental factors are also thought to be important in developing dyslexia, such as children's exposure to language prior to learning literacy (Pennington, 2002). This is likely to be especially important as the brain changes which give rise to phonological problems also seem to be connected to spoken language, although not to the processing of speech itself (Hulme & Snowling 1997).

Suggestions for which parts of the brain may be affected in phonological processing include the *word form area* at the visual rear of the brain, and the *perisylvian* region of the left hemisphere (Blakemore & Frith, 2005). They cite research by Eden that children with dyslexia do not appear to use the word form area in the way others do, utilising instead a different area – the parietal lobe – to integrate the sounds and pictures of words.

These processes are well described by Blakemore and Frith so will not be explored in detail here. However, as can be seen, the suggestion that genes 'cause' brain problems to result in dyslexia might give a somewhat pathological impression of this problem. One of the findings of the study, described in Chapter 9, is that it may be possible to interpret gene-environment interactions in a way which does not suggest gene or brain 'faults', but rather allows us to understand what children with different genetic identities – i.e. who are *different* rather than 'flawed' – might need in their environments and/or when learning to read.

The theory put forward by phonological core deficit researchers is that dyslexia is a manifestation of a deficient process of phonological de-coding due to an interaction between genes and the child's environment. These include parenting attitude (amount of spoken language or reading material around the home), nutritional factors, birth experiences and vaccinations, for example. But, as previously mentioned, it also includes the type of reading programme being taught as this is culturally decided, either as educational policy or within the school. Of course, the environment can also provide the help that is given to children in programmes aimed at helping dyslexia and so help mitigate any genetic 'risk'.

Phonological Teaching

It is generally considered best to design a tailor-made programme for the individual child, which reflects their own abilities and incorporates a range of skills needed in reading and writing. As reading skills develop, guided oral repeated reading is found to be more helpful than simply practicing silent reading. It is recommended that, with any literary programme, the younger the child the more effective the intervention is likely to be and there may in fact be a critical period for intervention with literary programmes (Fawcett, 2002). It is agreed that providing an 'at risk' child with support in their early school years, prior to the child 'failing' in school, would be the ideal, but there is as yet no single agreed early assessment procedure or programme of help available to all children in all schools. Parents consequently frequently search out their own solutions outside of the educational setting, sometimes in harness with the school's individualised programme for the child, but frequently not.

Other Theories of Dyslexia

Until recently the phonological core deficit hypothesis was the consensus view of the majority of researchers but recently other theories have been suggested. While generally accepting that phonological problems are the fundamental deficit in dyslexia, these researchers believe there may be another explanation for them. In the cerebellar theory, Nicolson and Fawcett (1999) argue that phonological problems may be the result of an impairment of the cerebellum. This is a part of the brain which is active in the acquisition of new skills and any motor/movement or cognitive/thinking task which becomes automatic, such as reading, spelling and phonological skills. They found children with dyslexia had a high incidence of cerebellar impairment. This also manifests itself in non-literary ways such as in balance difficulties and could also interfere with acquiring language dexterity. For example, if an infant has a cerebellar impairment, this might first show as a mild motor difficulty. The infant will be slower to sit up and walk and may have greater problems with fine muscle control such as in articulation and co-articulation. The infant might therefore be slower to babble and then to talk as these two activities appear to be connected in infant left-brain hemisphere development (Ramsay, 1984).

Even after speech has begun, the infant might be less fluent and 'dextrous' which will use up those mental resources within the brain that would otherwise have been available for processing feedback through the senses, such as the phonemes of language. This could lead to early deficits in phoneme awareness and prevent the automaticity which usually comes with learning a new skill. These researchers provide a fuller account of this developmental process and of how they tested their hypothesis through non-linguistic tasks in their 1999 paper. Because the main deficits they found in children with dyslexia were not just in their phonological skills but also in word-naming speed and balance, the cerebellar deficit hypothesis probably subsumes the phonological core deficit theory.

The Processing of Rapid Time

According to Nicolson and Fawcett, the cerebellar-impairment hypothesis can also account for the other major theory proposed to explain phonological problems in dyslexia. This is the *rapid temporal processing deficit*. Since the mid 1970's researchers have found children with dyslexia experience problems when rapidly naming or recalling letters, numbers, colours, or sounds. There also appeared to be a relationship between the severity of the speed problem and the individual's reading impairment. However, it is not their reaction to the stimuli that appears to be problematic, but the need to make a decision when presented with a choice, which causes the reduction in speed and therefore their response. Children with dyslexia appear to have a reduced ability to discriminate between incoming stimuli, including between consonants with similar acoustic frequencies. Physical differences have been found in the magnocellular (large cell) pathway of the Thalamus. This area of the brain is responsible for transmitting all incoming sensory information in both the visual and auditory streams,

These findings led several researchers to propose that a *temporal processing deficit* including those of discrimination between similar phoneme-sounds, might be the cause of the problems in dyslexia (Stein, 2001; Livingstone et.al, 1991; Galaburda, Menard & Rosen, 1994).

But, although this theory can explain some of the observed phonological difficulties, many researchers remain unconvinced that it can explain others, such as the inability to break words down into their constituent phonemes, or in detecting rhyme, both of which are present in children with dyslexia. This is partly why Nicolson and Fawcett consider the cerebellar hypothesis to encapsulate both the phonological core deficit and temporal processing theories. Phonological researchers, on the other hand, do not consider the non-literary difficulties of dyslexia to come under the umbrella of 'dyslexia'. They focus only on the literary problem itself. Consequently, the phonological core deficit theory explains some of what is understood about the development of reading but leaves some questions unanswered. Although the suggestion is that dyslexic children process phonemes differently from other readers, the other problems many dyslexic children exhibit, such as balance, rapid time processing of auditory and visual stimuli, and co-ordination problems are not well accounted for by this theory. Interestingly, Snowling and Hulme (1994) who are strong proponents of the theory, suggest that children who already have well-established phonological representations before literacy are well placed to make the necessary visual/sound associations of reading. This would mean that it is probably the child's younger language experience, where these representations develop, which is the key. A somewhat similar idea was proposed by Olson et.al. (1985) who suggested that dyslexia is a developmental delay in which children with dyslexia are 'behind' in acquiring phoneme code-knowledge, rather than 'brain impaired' as such. The phonological theory does not itself explore either of these latter two suggestions.

Multisensory Programmes

Although phoneme processing is the main focus in programmes for children with dyslexia, an older approach, originally developed by Edith Norrie in the 1940s, emphasises the importance of a *multisensory approach* (Hornsby 1984; Miles 1989; Combley 2001). Multisensory literary approaches may also focus on phonemes but do so by utilising simultaneous sensory techniques, sometimes known as V-A-K-T (visual, auditory, kinaesthetic, tactile) where several senses are brought into the reading exercise *simultaneously*. The child may listen to the sound and feel the movement by tracing letters, or hold a three-dimensional 'Norrie' letter. Multisensory programmes may also teach writing with reading so that tracing letters can be incorporated (Fernald, 1943). Some of these programmes are based on Gillingham-Stillman's (1946/1969) original recommendations, but have developed their own differences depending upon the practitioner's own background. For example *Hickey's Language Course* (Combley, 2001) focuses on written-language, whereas Hornsby and Shear (1975) are speech therapists and so in *Alpha to Omega*, they stress oral language as the starting point. Other multisensory programmes, such as the *Bangor Dyslexia Teaching System* (Miles, 1989) developed independently. There are a large number of multisensory programmes which, as Miles suggests, vary only in the structure and/or order in which they teach elements. Multisensory reading programmes are found to be of particular benefit to those whose dyslexia is severe.

The Theory Behind Multisensory Programmes

Despite its wide application the theoretical background for multisensory teaching is not fully developed. Practitioners use it because it appears to work and explanations for how they do so vary among them. Generally, each child is assumed to have 'stronger' or 'weaker' senses, being more 'visual' or more 'auditory'. Multisensory learning is considered to be diagnostic of the particular 'weak' sense and to possess a corresponding learning preference (auditory or visual). The child can be seen to demonstrate more confidence in their stronger area and to falter in the less favoured or 'weaker' sense. This could impede their ability to become literate, as it prevents the child from gaining automaticity or 'synthesis' of their sensory facilities, resulting in dyslexia. As previously suggested, by the time they have become of an age to commence literacy, children have refined sound-awareness, made by 'mapping' speech sounds to their associations. Dyslexic children, however, form 'fuzzy' connections between the senses which prevents these associations being made. It is thought that this 'fuzzy' mapping can be improved by multisensory teaching, which emphasises *simultaneous* stimulation of the senses involved.

Work on different senses has always been important in dyslexia research. Indeed the original theory was that dyslexia was a visual problem resulting in 'word-blindness' (or visual confusion of words). Stanovich (1993) although a strong promoter of the phonological impairment hypothesis, believes visual processing deficits may occur alongside the phonological in some individuals with dyslexia while Hanley (1997) reported students with no significant phonological difficulties, but significant visual ones, while other practitioners such as Tomatis and Berard concentrate on improving auditory processing alone. As long ago as 1962 Birch proposed that, rather than any single sense, a sensory integration problem may underlie dyslexia. However, findings from these experiments were inconclusive (Bryant, 2005) as they could have been explained by the 'single sense' alternative. Consequently, when in the late 1970s research evidence began to converge on phonological processing problems, this theory took over as the most likely explanation. Multisensory teaching still lacks a clear explanation for its efficacy, and its practice is based more on historical, empirical, practice which has found it to be successful, rather than on research explaining exactly why this might be.

Provision of Literary Programmes

In the UK intervention programmes have usually included a range of phonological skills and multisensory activities formed into 'hybrid' schemes. Some, such as that piloted in Cumbria schools (Hatcher et al 1994) incorporate tracing letter shapes and other play-based activities into a phonics-based programme, *Reading Recovery* (Clay 1987). The Cumbria Intervention, like some other programmes is also used with all poor readers and not just those assessed as dyslexic. At present there is no single programme used in all schools. This is largely due to there being no agreed theory which can account for dyslexia and how best to approach it. Understandably, proponents for different theories tend to disagree and challenge each other's findings. This has made the field of dyslexia research somewhat conflicted. For example, it is still difficult for many to accept that a non-literary programme may be helpful in a reading problem. Those who do not view dyslexia as purely a phoneme processing deficit, but who encompass the other problems of general timing, motor skill and balance, are consequently more likely to be open to non-literary programmes.

Non-Literary Programmes

Non-Literary programmes are frequently seen as 'unconventional' or even 'controversial' simply because they are not literary. It appears to some beyond explanation why anything other than a reading programme would be of use for a reading problem. However, as can be seen from Table 1 below there are a great many of them. So in addition to the abundance of literary programmes the parent of a child with dyslexia is offered a wide range of other approaches outside of school.

Non-literary programmes range from those which focus on single senses such as the auditory or visual programmes, to those utilising movement, dietary supplementation or medical drugs. While most educationalists are mainly concerned with how to teach the child with dyslexia, some of those whose programmes are non-literary attempt to remediate the problem at the level of the 'underlying causation'. Some non-literary programmes even suggest a cure is possible by their approach, something the established expertise on dyslexia does not currently accept. For example, guidance for parents frequently adopts the following tone in warning parents:

"When there is no effective cure for a condition, numerous dubious

Table 1. Some non-literary programmes for dyslexia

Some Non-Literary Programmes:	
Guy Berard Auditory Programme	Eurythmy
Bright Star	Kodaly Singing Programme
Arrow Method	*Piracetam*/antihistamines)
Tomatis Method	*Efalex* Essential Fatty Acid Supplementation
Bakker's Balance Model	Stein's Occlusion/overlays
Johansen Sound Therapy (JST)	Irlen's Lenses
Brain Net	Music-Making
Brain Gym	Primary Reflex Inhibition (PRI)
Perceptual Enrichment Programme (PEP	Handle Institute Method

'cures' arise. The existence of a number of so-called cures is usually a sign that no single one is effective' (Selikowitz, 1998).

This writer goes on to suggest such treatments are a waste of time and money; may be harmful to the physical and psychological well-being of the child and/or have detrimental effects on the family as a whole. Although one can find little evidence for these claims there is a certain aversion among some to non-literary programmes.

This is probably because they lie outside of the control of established educational delivery – where dyslexia is considered an educational problem – and are not necessarily in agreement with the standard perception of what is possible with children with dyslexia. The various organisations offering support and information to people with dyslexia also carry warnings. These are largely due to the fear that such programmes may offer 'false hope' to parents. But, given the debates and controversies within the field of dyslexia, the proliferation of literary programmes of all sorts and the lack of an agreed, consistent approach in schools, it is hardly surprising if parents themselves become confused and go in search of the optimum approach for their child.

Theories Underlying Non-Literary Programmes

All poor readers -whether dyslexic or not – show phonological processing problems, but many dyslexic children show additional signs including poor attention and concentration, language difficulties, and the balance and motor skills problems described earlier. Some researchers feel that without understanding the underlying cause of the whole problem, it will be hard to establish the strengths and weaknesses of the individual child and design the best approach to teaching poor readers of any sort (Nicolson, 2005). Nicolson, a proponent of the cerebellar hypothesis, goes on to suggest that with over 5 million dyslexic people in the UK it is unlikely that all will have the same underlying cause. But if 50% show balance problems, and are therefore likely to have a cerebellar impairment, that is 1.5 million who can be helped with programmes which work on establishing good cerebellar connections (2005, p659). Others claim that poor magnocellular pathways can be improved through nutritional supplementation with essential fatty acids (EFAs). Alex Richardson and Michael Crawford have spent many years researching the role of EFAs in developmental problems, and believe them vital to brain development. If supplementing with EFAs enables sensory stimuli to be transmitted through the brain more efficiently, making better links, then it is logical to provide these as well as a good reading programme. And, despite the warnings issued to parents, non-literary programmes are generally seen as complementary to good teaching strategies because, if a child is to become literate, at some point she or he will need to learn to read and write.

The Study

While the sheer diversity of programmes may be confusing to parents or of concern to researchers, educators and dyslexic organisations, it does nevertheless raise an important question. This is: How can all these different programmes be helpful? Against the backdrop of diversity, and coming to the field of dyslexia with no prior knowledge or experience of practice or research, I found this the most significant aspect. In the following research study I sought to understand whether diverse but successful programmes might be connected through a 'common active ingredient' and, if this shared element could be discovered so as to provide a deeper understanding of the causes and best practice for children with dyslexia.

Programmes Included in The Study

The 14 programmes were classified according to their focus, as follows:

Auditory:	Tomatis Method
	Johansen Sound Therapy
	Bakker's Balance Model
Visual:	Stein's Occlusion and Colour Overlays
	Irlen's Colour Filters
Movement:	*Brain Gym*
	Primary Reflex Inhibition
	Dore/DDAT Exercise Programme
Multisensory:	*Alpha-Omega* Literacy Programme
	Music-Making
	Ron Davis Method
Pharmacological:	Pharmaceutical Drugs
	Efalex Essential Fatty Acid Supplementation
Phonological:	*Phono-Graphix*

An outline of each of these 14 programmes is provided in Chapters 2-7, followed in Chapter 8 by a detailed account of how the study was carried out and, in Chapter 9, an examination of the findings.

CHAPTER 2

AUDITORY PROGRAMMES

Three different types of auditory stimulation were included: the Tomatis Method, Johansen Sound Therapy and Bakker's Balance Model. Although each has some similarity with the other two, they have very different theoretical positions.

1   The Tomatis Method

Theory
Alfred Tomatis was a French surgeon, neurologist and ENT specialist whose work with opera singers led him to formulate *Audio-Psycho-Phonology*. In this the ear is said to have three main functions:

a)   The ear provides energy to the brain for it to convert sounds, perceived vibration and bodily movements into electrical impulses. The ear alone provides over 80% of the sensory stimulation the brain receives.

b)   The ear provides a sense of spatial awareness and control of movement and posture through the vestibular (balance) system within it.

c)   Hearing is only the third function, which appears at a later
       date than the first two functions.

The brain matures as a result of all the stimulation received by the ear, which is why its early development is significant. The sense of spatial awareness, for example, starts within the first few weeks in the womb and the ear is totally mature at only 4.5 months of pregnancy. In contrast it takes 42 years for the brain to fully mature. Tomatis believes we 'read with our ears' (1972/91, p58) and when the functions of the ear have not developed as they should the child is unable to translate his own thoughts into inner-communication. He suggests a relationship forms in the womb between the child and the mother's voice, and that this relationship must be established *in utero* or language will not develop very well and sometimes may not develop at all. After birth this relationship continues as speech becomes more complex and meaningful. If the mother/child relationship fails to evolve Tomatis believes language integration will stagnate and the normal linguistic structures will not take place. The child will become 'dyslexic' even before s/he has come into contact with the written word and, because of the ear's role in spatial relationships and the vestibular system, this will also show as the coordination problems observed in children with dyslexia.

The Stages of Listening Development
Tomatis describes how the newborn child gradually opens up to the world of airborne sound waves. The unborn baby is tuned initially to the fluid environment of the womb. During delivery there occurs what Tomatis calls a *sonic birth* where the outer and middle ear are forced to adapt to the pressure of air around them. Because the middle ear and Eustachian Tube retain their amniotic fluid for ten days, the ear initially remains tuned to pre-birth frequencies. 10 days after birth everything alters and the amniotic fluid begins to recede. The middle ear must now adjust to full air-borne acoustics. This adaption has an impact on the entire development of the child.

The child progresses through chatter, imitation and speech until reaching some independence at about 3-4 years old. Tomatis perceives this as a broadening of the social life, which is symbolised for him by the increasing role of the father in the child's world. If this encounter with the social world is successful, security and calm are established and the child is able to step out towards the wider world. Thus, this greater socialisation depends entirely upon the path from the womb. Tomatis believes this development can be greatly impaired by communication difficulties with the parents. It is thought particularly important that the child experience the high-frequency sound of the mother's voice.

Brain Laterality
Laterality, dominance or advantage are equivalent terms used by practitioners to distinguish sidedness – left or right – of the brain/body. As can be seen in Figure 3 below, the neuronal pathways from each ear travel to the opposite (contra-lateral) brain hemisphere for processing, although there are also weaker same-side (ipsi-lateral) pathways not shown on the diagram:

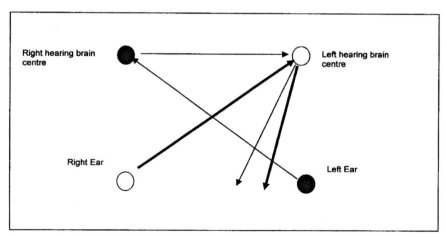

Fig 3. Auditory Pathways

The left-brain hemisphere is specialised for language and sound in most people and auditory stimulation travels more quickly from the right ear to the left-brain, as the neural pathway is shorter than from the left ear to the right brain. The left recurrent nerve branch of the Vagus Nerve in the ear is also longer. Tomatis therefore believes the right ear must be dominant (lateralised) for hearing if the correct inner communicative pathways are to develop in the child. However, this does not mean that left-handed children will be made to become right handed, but only that right-ear dominance is the aim of the treatment.

Tomatis states that the newborn infant listens to his/her mother first with their left ear as, when held, the right ear is usually against the mother's heart. This means that in the newborn it is usually the right hemisphere that is active first and the left hemisphere (which is stimulated by the right ear) develops later. The developmental transfer from a 1:1 mother/child relationship to wider social-involvement usually occurs at between 3-5 years of age, depending on the child. However, Tomatis believes children may suffer 'traumas' of a physical or emotional nature, which could in effect keep the child 'stuck' in right brain hemisphere function, thus suspending other areas of development. Alternatively, the child may be thrown 'forward' into premature left-brain hemisphere functioning, again interfering with their development.

Dyslexia itself is perceived as merely a symptom of a range of problems, including: incorrectly acquired language, inadequate body awareness, incorrect spatio-temporal organization and incorrect personal integration within the environment. Possible reasons given by Tomatis for why the mother/child relationship may be disturbed include premature birth or difficult delivery, or the altered role of mothers in society resulting in many babies having insufficient time with their mothers.

Practice

The remediation programme aims to re-establish the 'correct' developmental 3-stage sequence of hearing by replicating the child's experience of his/her mother's voice before, during and after birth, or by using high frequency music to replicate this effect:

> "We use the Electronic Ear to take him back over the road he should have followed, from the moment of his conception onwards." (Tomatis 1972/91, p145)

Tomatis holds that the place for diagnosis is pre-school and that waiting for reading to show problems is leaving it very late. However, he believes teachers would easily be able to undertake assessment of children in school using his assessment method.

A   Assessment

In the assessment a series of tests together known as *The Listening Test*, are undertaken which highlight ear dominance and also show where inner conflicts from trauma are located in the body. The individual's ability to hear at a specific pre-determined intensity threshold is measured using frequencies of the normal sound scale ranging from 125-8000 hz (frequency as cycles per second). Conduction curves from the ear canal and mastoid bone provide a graph which shows whether sonic distortions are present. The two curves it creates will be parallel in unaffected children but not those with dyslexia. Base modulations range from 125-800 hz, in the middle range from 800-2000 hz and in the treble range from 2000-8000 hz. Next, the child's ability for auditory discrimination and integration is measured. Tomatis believes this discriminatory ability varies according to age:

"In the dyslexic, ability to distinguish variations within this range (125 hz to 8000 hz) is extremely disturbed. Suppression of treble tones is a constant.

We could say that these children are 'colour blind' when it comes to the tonal values of sound." (Tomatis 1972, p124)

The child's temporal spatial orientation is then tested. Tomatis believes that a dyslexic child cannot easily locate him/herself in the universe and this test shows their degree of confusion in localising ability. Finally, the leading ear/auditory laterality evaluation takes place while s/he listens to sound. This identifies which ear is acting as dominant.

Listening Therapy
Using the test results, an individual programme is designed to re-establish correct listening with right-ear dominance. The aim of treatment is to stimulate the desire to listen and to re-establish the developmentally correct series of acoustics through which the ear must pass before, during and following birth. Although the right ear is the focus the left ear is not ignored, but it does not receive equal stimulation. The result is the establishment of 'optimal hearing' across the full range of thresholds and frequencies as measured by the *Optimal Hearing Curve* (OHC) shown in Fig. 4. This 're-tuning' is based on the concept

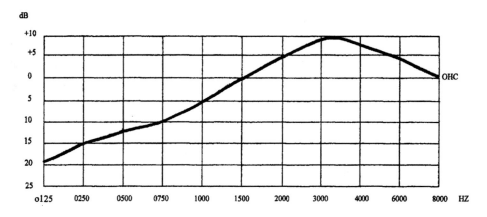

Fig 4. The Optimal Hearing Curve

that the child needs to focus more on the higher frequencies (presented by the mother's voice or music) and less on the lower, background ones. The consonants which make up language sounds are also higher frequencies, whereas background sounds are lower. Therefore tuning the ear to pick up higher frequencies in this way also enables word sounds to be more easily distinguished

Filtered Sounds

The *Electronic Ear* is adapted for each child and is used to reproduce the 'perfect ear'. It comprises microphone, amplifiers, filters and earphones and consists principally of two channels joined by an electronic relay that progressively condition the child's ear until audition becomes better adjusted across the whole range of sound to include the previously missing higher frequencies. The *Electronic Ear* contains two filters, enabling high and low frequency sounds to be filtered to the child. This process exercises the middle ear and the two tiny bones, stirrup and hammer, which absorb and block background sound enabling clear listening. There are three developmental steps: the child in the womb, the child/mother dyad and from c.3/4 years of age, the child/social relationship (represented by the father).

B   Treatment

The programme teaches the child to hear sounds as heard by individuals who are not dyslexic. They acquire the normal auditory posture possessed by those who hear correctly and who have therefore been able to structure normal relational networks for themselves. The treatment first utilises the mother's voice as heard by the child in the womb to replicate the pre-natal acoustic environment. Tomatis states these awaken memory traces and the desire for the relationship with the mother. He says:

"We have to go all the way back to the uterine environment,

or at least to an approximation of it, in order to recover this."
(Tomatis 1972, p145)

When use of the mother's voice is not possible, the training is done using filtered music. This *must* be rich in treble tones and is usually Mozart or Gregorian chants. This stage of the treatment culminates in the *sonic birth* which replicates the child's birth or transition from hearing the mother's voice through fluid to air.

Sonic Birth

This is achieved by using the mother's voice filtered from 8000 hz to 100 hz. Tomatis stresses how important it is not to lose the feeling of the intimate relationship the child now has with his/her mother, experienced during the final months in the womb. When the 'birth' has been re-created the mother's voice is used to reproduce the sonic experience at 10 days. During the treatment the child will gradually re-adjust to an acoustic environment of air, instead of fluid, and begin a new phase of his/her relationship with the mother out of the womb. The mother's voice in air is played through headphones to the child with interludes of music, in particular Mozart, to enable the ear to fully open to listening. There may be 10-20 sessions on this stage before the next is appropriate.

Active Phase

Following this the third and final *active phase* commences where the child leaves behind the 'passive' stage of listening and enters into two-way dialogue. This prepares the child for social communication and involves training the child, through listening, for entrance into a verbal relationship with his/her environment. The transfer from left-ear to right-ear dominance is complete and encounters with others, symbolised by the father, can successfully take place. (To use the father's voice in the early stages of the treatment is considered upsetting to the child.) The child's participation is required during this phase of the training as s/he is asked to repeat what has been heard through the *Electronic Ear*. While these different sound treatments are being focussed directly to the child through earphones, s/he relaxes with light activities such as drawing or jigsaw puzzles.

A typical treatment programme might consist of: 2 weeks listening therapy; 3-5 weeks break; 1 week listening therapy; 5-7 weeks break; 1 week listening therapy; 12 weeks break; 1 week listening therapy. The rest periods between sessions are considered crucial, as the brain will alter organically during these to accommodate the stimulation provided by the therapy. Further information including case studies can be found at: www.tomatis.com

II   Johansen's Sound Therapy (JST)

Theory

Johansen Sound Therapy (JST) – also known as Hemisphere Specific Auditory Stimulation (HSAS) – presents a different form of acoustic treatment. It was developed in Denmark by Dr. Kjeld Johansen, Director of the Baltic Dyslexia Research Laboratory, from original work by Christian A. Volf. Johansen's view is that many children with language difficulties have problems *processing language*. Their ability to take in, organise, store, retrieve, add to existing information and express what they want to say, is weak. Auditory processing disorders can affect development of speech, language and communication as well as reading and spelling, resulting in problems with talking and understanding and/or dyslexia and other learning difficulties. This problem may be inherited or develop as a result of repeated bouts of hearing loss or reduced hearing levels in one or both ears due, for example, to 'glue ear' or regular ear infections. However, Johansen suggests there are many children for whom there is no obvious reason for their difficulty.

Left-Ear Dominance in Dyslexic Children

The programme is based on Johansen's research finding that dyslexia is associated with some combination of right-handedness, right-footedness and right-eyedness in the presence of left-earedness. The risk of being dyslexic is given as 10/12 for an individual with this combination and 4/15 for an individual with these four preferences all to the right, (Johansen, 1994). Usually, around the time of their fourth birthday, most children demonstrate right-ear advantage towards linguistic stimuli, although this is a question of degree.

Where language is poorly organised a child will have to work hard to unravel what is said and may be unable to sustain the level of concentration required to do so, thus affecting learning. Generally, those with reading disabilities such as dyslexia have early and continuous auditory problems. Larsen (1989) and Oyler and Matkin (1987) found the number of children having right-ear impairment and school problems was five times as great as the number having left-ear impairment and school problems. Jensen and colleagues (1989) tested thirty children (aged 10-16) suffering from unilateral hearing loss. Their results showed that right ear impaired children performed significantly poorer than their left ear impaired counterparts. While 95% of the left-ear impaired had satisfactory academic progress only 45.5% of the right-ear impaired managed school without problems.

Whilst most people have right-ear dominance with corresponding left brain hemisphere location for language, a very small percentage have all functions on the left side of the body (and corresponding right-hemisphere dominance) and so are 'left-eared'. In nearly 30% of the population the dominances are more uncertain (Springer & Deutsch, 1981). Johansen believes left-ear auditory dominance more than left-handedness, left-footedness or left-eyedness is a key indicator of dyslexia.

He consequently agrees with Tomatis that the quickest and most efficient way for language information to reach the processing area in the left hemisphere is via the right ear (as shown in Fig. 3, p19). Inconsistent or left ear preference can therefore adversely affect the learning of language and its organisation within the brain.

As a result, sounds within words (phonemes) words themselves or even whole sentences may be jumbled or in the wrong sequence. This in turn may affect the understanding and production of both speech and writing. JST aims, as does the Tomatis Method, to rectify this by altering auditory dominance to the right ear (left-brain hemisphere) or by establishing this where there is no fixed dominance.

Brain Plasticity
JST depends upon the concept of brain plasticity. This is the term used for the ability of the brain to grow new nerve connections, (dendrites and synapses) in response to stimulation from the environment. Whereas it used to be thought that brain cells died off and were not replaced, it is now understood that the brain can always grow and that in early childhood it is particularly flexible or *plastic*. Johansen believes there is a link between a lack of sensory stimulation of the auditory system in the young child and altered cell size in the magnocellular nerve pathway (the medial geniculate nuclei) of the thalamus of the brain. The thalamus is the major relay centre for sensory information, including that from the ears and eyes. Most of the sensory relay nuclei of the thalamus transmit to the cerebellum and the appropriate areas of the cortex, so any lack of sensory stimulation would mean the number of dendrites and the branching and number of synapses of brain connection pathways to and between auditory centres was reduced. This sensory deprivation may then lead to altered auditory laterality for some or all sound-frequencies in the language spectrum. Such auditory deprivation, for whatever reason, may induce dyslexia (or spelling and reading problems

indistinguishable from dyslexia). However, because of its plasticity, improvements in brain connections may also be induced in children by using special auditory stimulation techniques such as JST.

Listening Tests

This model utilises binaural testing, where both ears are sent sounds simultaneously, as well as pure-tone monaural (one ear at a time) testing. Monaural testing gives hearing thresholds for each ear separately, which are compared with the Tomatis Optimum Hearing Curve, shown in Fig 4. Binaural pure-tone dichotic listening tests (BPTA) can detect confusion or inconsistency in ear dominance. Pure sounds are sent randomly to right, left, or both ears simultaneously through an audiometer and headphones, adjusted for tone and/or volume. These establish normal monaural threshold measurements and also show divergence between right and left ear auditory function. Another binaural method, the dichotic listening test, (DL) is used to monitor linguistic sounds (words, syllables, and/or non-words). Johansen suggests that screening for auditory laterality by BPTA and DL testing reveals a highly distinct deviation between the results for normal readers and those for children with dyslexia, regardless of sex and age, but to a certain degree dependent on handedness. From his studies, Johansen found dyslexic children often have much greater divergences between their thresholds than other groups. Furthermore, the hearing of the left ear in the dyslexic children was more often than not the most sensitive. Johansen concludes:

> "With total or partial left-ear advantage, phonemes or portions of phonemes will be perceived through the left ear while other portions will be perceived through the right ear. Due to the neural construction of the auditory system in which the contra-lateral auditory input arrives at the auditory nerve's cortical endpoint prior to ipsilateral input and (in the

case of the left hemisphere at least) provokes a stronger reaction, total or partial left-sided auditory laterality can mean that portions of certain phonemes are mixed obscuring the difference between 'b' and 'p' or 'd' and 't' for example." (1991, p11)

An individual's ear dominance can also be disturbed by the intensity of a sound. Everyday vocal speech communication rarely supersedes 50 decibels (dB). A whispering voice level is approximately 20 dB. Berlin (1977) found during experiments with verbal stimuli that at a general sound level of 80 dB, an increase of 15 dB for the left ear meant the shift of laterality to this ear. At 50 dB the level for the left ear only needed to be increased by 5dB in order to attain left ear advantage for synchronous signals. Johansen states:

"– it is precisely this discrepancy in sensitivity of 5 dB in the left ear's favour over a more or less limited frequency range which seems to be characteristic for many dyslexics" (1988, p8).

And, under certain stress-related influences such as when a poor speller is forced to write down his/her answers, ear dominance may also alter (Johansen, 1991, p.3.).

Higher Frequencies
JST utilises the Optimal Hearing Curve (OHC) to re-tune the hearing and enable better focus on the higher frequencies than the lower. This is also where the consonants of speech are located. These consonants allow us to recognize words and give them their individuality. Vowels are longer in duration and acoustically simpler, meaning that consonants are more vulnerable to disturbances and loss than vowels, especially if the consonants are initially perceived in the 'wrong' cerebral hemisphere.

Practice

A   Assessment Procedure

Initially, students go through a visual, handedness and auditory test battery. This contains dichotic listening with language sounds (syllables or words) and dichotic listening with 11 pure tones 125-8000 hz – both at the 20 dB level and at threshold levels – plus a one-minute assessment of hearing thresholds.

B   Treatment

Based on this assessment two or more individually customised music tapes are recorded for each child from a master CD: 'Syncrosound Music' by Bent-Peder Holbech. On the basis of the child's audiogram of monaudio-thresholds the graphic equalizer is adjusted before recording to compensate for the deviations from the Optimum Hearing Curve. The compensations used are 40% of the deviation and never to exceed +/- 12dB. These tapes are played for up to 15 minutes per day initially for 16-30 weeks and can be listened to at any time through headphones, on a personal stereo, or music centre. It is hoped to obtain about 25-50 hours of listening by the end of a 6-month period. The programme lasts for approximately 9 months although the time required to achieve an Optimal Hearing Curve will vary. Auditory re-assessments may be performed every 6th- 8th week and if indicated a new tape is recorded after each assessment. Full information on Johansen Sound Therapy can be found at:

www.dyslexia-lab.dk (Baltic lab)

www.johansensoundtherapy.com

III   Bakker's Balance Model

Theory

D.J Bakker formulated his *Balance Model of Dyslexia* in 1995. He is credited with bringing into clinical practice the accumulated knowledge of nearly seventy years of research into the relationship between dyslexia and cerebral/brain organisation. In the early stages, learning reading and/or writing has a predominantly visuo-perceptual analysis, which allows new or unfamiliar material to be recognised for later processing. Bakker postulated that the active exploration of shapes and contours of letters and words in these initial stages of reading primarily involves right brain-hemisphere functioning. This is because of its superior visuo-spatial ability, processing of inter-modal information, association of word shapes, sound and meaning, and the formation of reference systems necessary for written language. Then, once a frame of reference has been developed and as the reading process advances, with increased analysis of and syntheses of text, the contribution of the left hemisphere becomes more salient. Therefore, a switch in hemispheric control must take place at some point during the development of the reading process. In c.66% of children this is thought to be between two months of beginning formal reading instruction and the end of first grade in school at 4-5 years (Kappers & Hamburger (1994).

Bakker's studies suggested that proficient reading shows either a *lack* of ear dominance or left-ear (right-hemisphere) dominance in younger children, but becoming right-ear (left-hemisphere) dominant at older ages. This reflects the child's developmental progression from right hemisphere to left hemisphere (i.e. balanced) functioning. For those children who do not make this shift Bakker proposed two types of dyslexia, dependent upon which hemisphere was under-functioning:

1   L-type. Which is present when the beginning reader
     prematurely relies on left hemisphere linguistic reading
     strategies surpassing the preliminary stage of right
     hemisphere visuo-spatial processing.

2   P-type. Which exists where correct processing of text by the
     right hemisphere occurs from the beginning of reading but
     then there is a failure to switch to the more complex left-
     hemisphere strategies in later reading.

Practice

As in JST, Bakker's treatment programme rests on the assumption that
the brain is *plastic*, in that it is able to develop new connections in
response to stimulation. Indeed, Bakker used the term 'ecological' about
this model, meaning by this that the brain develops from interaction with
its environment. As Lorusso says:

> "A major assumption underlying the use of hemisphere
> stimulation procedures is that functional brain organisation
> is flexible and modifiable, originating from and influenced
> by interaction with the environment." (Lorusso, 1994, p14)

Bakker undertook systematic treatment studies to attempt stimulation of
the cerebral hemisphere thought to be under-functioning during reading.
He formulated two distinct treatments for the L- and P-types. These
were: (1) hemispheric-specific stimulation methods (HSS) and (2)
hemispheric-alluding methods (HAS).

These treatment methods utilise mainly multi-sensory (auditory-
visual) stimuli, but also include tactile stimulation, although Kappers
and Hamburger say:

"It is not quite clear why addition of the tactile information channel in some cases gives better results". (Kappers and Hamburger 1994, p107)

A   *Assessment*

Before the application of treatment the child is assessed in order to be classified, in the first place as dyslexic and secondly to discover if s/he is either L- or P-type. For this the diagnostic assessment 'key approach' is followed. The criteria for this include: a) a reading and spelling lag of at least 2 years compared to age level; b) normal intelligence; c) an unexpected discrepancy between expected and realised achievement in reading and spelling; d) the reading disability is independent from and not caused by other handicaps; e) a delayed disturbed development of language and, in many cases, f) familial occurrence. In order to fully establish whether L- or P-type is indicated the following are identified:

1)   What type of reading error dominates, substantive (SE) or time-consuming (TC)?

2)   What type of strategy is dominant, a hurried-inaccurate or a slow-accurate one?

3)   Is the reading skill on a level that, on average, is thought to be consistent with the predominantly left hemispheric or right hemispheric control?

4)   How many reading sub-skills are insufficiently developed?

Sub-skills are the skills required before literacy can be learned. They include the ability to scan from left to right (for English); the ability to match visual symbols to their auditory sounds; the ability to blend sound units (phonemes) into words; the ability to break down words into their sound units; the understanding that sometimes two or more letters can represent the same sound, and that most sounds can be represented in more than one way. These four points are used to make a decision on which hemisphere should have priority in treatment, as shown in Table 2:

If the reading sub-skills are missing or insufficiently developed, reading level is not equivalent to that expected at Grade 1 and substantive errors dominate or, when reading strategy is hurried/inaccurate, the right hemisphere is stimulated (RH). For children where these criteria do not hold true, and who are reading at least on a level equivalent to that expected by the end of Grade 1 and/or make many time-consuming errors together with non-fluent or slow reading, left hemispheric stimulation will be indicated (LH).

Table 2. Hemisphere Assessment in Bakers Balance Model.

Pre-initial skills (sub-skills), initial reading skills and/or inaccurate, hasty reading:	⟶ RH
Accurate but slow reading:	⟶ LH

B   Treatment

The clinician will attempt to determine the root of the problem and the phase in the learning-to-read process in which problems arose. Where there is more than one root problem treatment begins with the developmentally 'oldest' one. The rationale of the treatment overall is one of assisting the weaker hemisphere rather than compensating through existing strengths.

HSS

The rehabilitation programme called Hemisphere-Specific Stimulation (HSS) is based on the crossed (contra-lateral) relationship between the left and right brain and body, in which the brain processes information from the opposite side of the body. It results from the manipulation of three important factors:

1   Two main sensory modalities are considered: visual and tactile. Only those pathways are stimulated which will activate the under-functioning hemisphere. In the visual modality, images (usually words) are projected to the visual hemi-field connected with the target hemisphere. In the tactile modality three-dimensional letters are presented to the fingers of the contra-lateral (opposite side) hand. In the standard treatment, the child's own reading voice may be played back to him/her through the ear co-lateral (same side) to the hemisphere to be stimulated, while music is sent to the other ear.

2   Various dimensions of material characteristic are manipulated, such as imageability, perceptual complexity, (typeface of words presented) presence or absence of illustrations etc, in order to activate visuo-spatial or linguistic strategies.

3   Finally, task instructions are designed in order to invoke
        particular strategies such as judging the physical
        characteristics of the words and matching them with other
        words, as opposed to completing sentences or words
        according to the semantic or syntactic structure of the
        material.

HAS Treatment

Hemisphere Alluding Stimulation (HAS) works by stimulating the non-
target hemisphere and was specifically designed for use in a school situation
but is also used in clinical settings. It usually involves manipulation of
material characteristics and task instructions. Whereas the left hemisphere is
invoked by manipulation of semantic/syntactic and phonetic properties of
texts, L-type dyslexics (those who have 'skipped' some right-hemisphere
stimulation) who are receiving right hemisphere stimulation HAS, might be
presented with perceptually demanding text to be read.

A computer program called 'Scrambler' is used to produce perceptually
demanding texts. An example is shown in Fig 5 below. These texts
accentuate the perceptual aspects as much as possible and suppress the
tendency to read in a rushed or hurried fashion.

In contrast, P-type children, (those remaining too long in right-hemisphere
function) who are receiving stimulation of left hemisphere HAS, might do
so via word and sentence completion and/or rhyming tasks (Lorusso, 1994).

A child being given HSS treatment for left hemisphere specific

ϙerceꝑtUᴧiLy cOmpLex texꞇ

Fig 5. Perceptually demanding text.

stimulation may gain from the addition of a left hemisphere-alluding program (HAS) as progress is made. S/he may, for example, be presented with texts from which words have been deleted and asked to supply suitable words to fill the gaps, based on their meaning and context, or asked to place randomly presented words in the right order to form a sentence. In all cases treatment is continually evaluated, altered and/or discontinued as the child develops, in order to keep pace with and further initiate improvement. Kappers and Hamburger (1994) provide a number of cases of children successfully treated with Bakker's Balance Model.

CHAPTER 3

VISUAL PROGRAMMES

Two different visual programmes were included in the study. A third, *BrightStar,* is discussed in relation to the study findings in Chapter 10. Again, although the two programmes appear similar in that both use overlays or lenses, they are un-alike in every other way.

I   Stein's Occlusion & Tinted Lenses

Theory
John Stein developed his work at the Laboratory of Physiology, Oxford University and the Learning Disability Clinic at the Royal Berkshire Hospital, Reading. In it he emphasises the role of the magnocellular system of the thalamus in dyslexia and, in particular, in spelling. The cerebellum, as the head ganglion of the magnocellular system, also plays an important role. A schematic relationship of the sub-organs of the brain can be seen in Fig. 6 on page 42.

Many researchers' work has led to an understanding of the cerebellum as crucial in acquiring all sensorimotor skills. In reading, this enables control of eye movements, mediates 'inner speech' for phonological awareness, calibrates visual motion signals and eye fixation. According to Stein the cerebellum is "– clearly defective in dyslexics" (2001, p13).

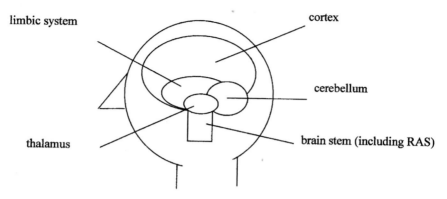

Fig. 6. Relationship of sub-sections of the brain

The Visual Magnocellular System

The magnocellular layer is so-called because 10% of the ganglion cells, whose axons provide the signals that pass from the eye to the rest of the brain, are noticeably larger (magno) than the remaining smaller (parvo) cells. This means they gather light from a larger area, so are more sensitive and faster reacting, but are not sensitive to fine detail or colour. The visual magnocellular system is responsible for timing visual events when reading. It signals any visual motion that occurs if unintended movements lead to images moving off the fovea of the eye ('retinal slip').

These signals are then used to bring the eyes back on target. Thus sensitivity to visual motion seems to help determine how well orthographic (spelling) skill can develop.

Visual magno cells project to the primary visual area in the rear of the brain (occipital cortex) through the main relay nucleus of the thalamus, the *lateral geniculate nucleus* (LGN). Visual information then flows from the primary visual cortex through a variety of pathways, which form two main streams: the dorsal and ventral streams. The dorsal stream is believed to be involved in the perception of 'where' objects are, and the ventral stream in 'what' objects are. The dorsal stream plays a major role in the visual guidance of eye and limb movements and projects onwards to the frontal eye fields, superior colliculus and cerebellum – all very important for visuo-motor controls. Although there is a mingling of magno and parvo inputs in the primary visual cortex, the dorsal visual processing stream is dominated by inputs from the magnocellular system. Stein suggests that an advantage of this separation of the visual magno and parvocellular systems is that their sensitivity can be assessed using stimuli that selectively activate one or other system.

The Magnocellular System in Dyslexics

In dyslexics the development of the visual magnocellular system is 'impaired'. The magnocellular layer of the LGN was found to be abnormal with its neurons being 30% smaller in area than that of non-dyslexics' brains. Their motion sensitivity is therefore reduced. Dyslexics' contrast sensitivity was also shown to be impaired compared to that of non-dyslexic controls, particularly at low spatial and high temporal frequencies where rapid processing of close-together stimuli is required. But, at high spatial frequencies which are mediated by the parvocellular system, they actually performed better than controls. Dyslexics also seemed to have smaller receptive fields generally. Stein concludes:

> "– majority opinion still has it that (inadequate development of phonological skill) is the main, if not the only problem from which dyslexics suffer and that visual disturbances are very rare. In contrast, we find that in only about a third of dyslexics are their main problems phonological; in about one third their main problems are visual/orthographic; and

the remaining third have both problems in almost equal proportions. But we think that even the phonological problems have a much more fundamental physiological cause (Stein, 2001,p23).

Binocular Control

One of the most important uses to which visual motion signals are put, is to achieve visual perceptual stability where both eyes focus (fixate) together on an object. This is achieved through the computational 'morphing' of sequential images from unintentional eye movements, and the correction of larger, unintended eye movements, by magnocellular feedback to visual motor systems from the retina. Two thirds of the children referred to Stein's *Learning Disabilities Clinic,* in the ophthalmic department of Reading Hospital, Berkshire, have unstable binocular control. Stein believes that good magnocellular function is essential for stable binocular fixation.

Unintended eye movements are a particular problem when the eyes are converged at 30 cm, the distance required for reading. Stein found most children with reading problems have markedly unsteady binocular fixation, which correlates with their visual perceptual instability. Hence the quality of their binocular fixation determines how steady the letters appear when they are trying to read them. A child's visual motion sensitivity consequently dictates their ability to determine the correct order of letters in a word. Children with low magnocellular function, as evidenced by reduced visual motion sensitivity, are slower and make more errors in judging the correct order of letters in words when briefly presented with neighbouring anagrams (Cornelissen et al, 1997). Being uncontrolled, the movements of the two eyes are not linked, nor monitored. The two lines of sight may therefore cross or re-cross and the usual feedback of motion signals (utrocular control) is absent.

Left Neglect

Another phenomenon associated with unstable binocular control is mild 'left visual- field neglect'. This can be seen in their drawings of clocks where a child may bunch all the figures to the right side and leave the left empty, as shown in Fig.7.

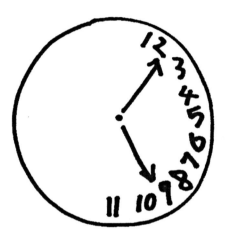

Fig 7. An Example of Left Neglect

Other Magnocellular Systems

All the sensory and motor systems have large (magno) cells specialised for temporal processing. Those in the auditory system, the medial geniculate nucleus (MGN) relay auditory signals to the auditory cortex of the brain. These track the frequency and amplitude changes for distinguishing phonemes. As with the visual magno cells, the MGN of dyslexics have been found to be disordered and smaller than in non-dyslexic brains (Galaburda, Menard & Rosen 1994). Dyslexics also have reduced tactile sensation consistent with impaired magnocellular dorsal column function. Stein concludes that magnocells in general might be affected in dyslexia and there may be some common underlying factor that determines the development of all magnocells throughout the brain. This is supported by Hockfield and Sur who found a common system of magnocellular neurones throughout the brain that express a common surface antigen which can be recognized by specific antibodies such as CAT 301. These are found not only in the visual system but in the auditory, somaesthetic (bodily sensational) and motor systems (cited in Stein, 2001, p27). Some of the heaviest staining with the magnocellular marker CAT 301 occurred in the Purkinje cells of the cerebellum. Because the cerebellum is the head ganglion of the magnocellular system, Stein gives this as further evidence for his theory.

Genes & Dyslexia

Like many others Stein believes there to be a clear genetic basis for the impaired development of magnocells throughout the brain, the best understood linkage being that to the region of the Major Histocompatibility Complex (MHC) Class 1 on the short arm of Chromosome 6. This helps to control the production of antibodies. Stein therefore suggests the development of magnocells may be impaired by auto-antibodies affecting the developing brain in the womb. Although no single genetic 'cause' of dyslexia has been found, many of the suggested chromosomal sites related to dyslexia, including the MHC on C6, are involved with immunological regulation. Stein suggests that as the feature that links all magnocells is their expression of common surface antigens, important for their recognition by other cells, they might be vulnerable to damage at the hands of a rogue auto-antibody that recognised that antigen.

Some evidence exists that mothers may develop antibodies to foetal magnocellular neurones, small quantities of which may, under some circumstances, cross the placenta and blood-brain barrier and damage the developing magnocells (Vincent et al, 2000). The production of such an antibody would be regulated by the MHC Class 1 system, since one of its most important functions is to distinguish 'self' from 'not-self' antigens. Also, it seems that this immune response is pressed into service during development to regulate the differentiation of magnocells:

> "In other words, this is probably the system that is responsible for directing the synthesis of antibodies against the foetus. But normally the placenta provides effective protection from them. It seems however, that vulnerability to such attack may be inherited in dyslexics, because they and their families seem to have more than their fair share of autoimmune diseases." (Stein, 2001, p29)

Consequently, Stein supports the importance of Essential Fatty Acids (fully described in Chapter 6) during pregnancy because:

> "– immune reactions mobilize polyunsaturated fatty acids (PUFAs) from cell membranes to provide precursors of the cytokines required for effective cellular responses to foreign material. Supplementation with these is then helpful to dyslexics." (Stein, 2001, p29)

Stein has proposed that the suggested genetic difference in dyslexia is an evolutionary adaption. However, this idea poses a mystery for him in that:

> "The magnocellular defect that I am outlining would definitely be a selective disadvantage – because it would undoubtedly be dangerous. Even a mild degree of insensitivity to visual motion would put you at risk of not seeing the advancing sabre toothed tiger quite early enough to avoid death." (Stein, 2001, p30)

While, on the positive side, he suggests that the stronger links between the parvo cells in dyslexic individuals might bind the processing together more efficiently than in ordinary brains. This could enable the holistic 'lateral thinking' and 'seeing the big picture' that great artists, politicians, entrepreneurs and many dyslexics display.

Practice

There are two forms of visual aid advocated by Stein:

a)   Monocular occlusion for visual sensory training

b)   Coloured filters/overlays during reading

a)   Monocular Occlusion

Because of their binocular instability, visual confusion may be exacerbated by the two eyes presenting different competing versions of where individual letters are situated. Hence using only one eye with the other blanked will often improve their reading. Simply blanking the vision of one eye can simplify the visual confusion and help these children to see the letters properly. In addition, it can enable the child's brain to establish a dominance pattern (usually the left hemisphere) and reduce confusion.

Treatment entails patching one eye – usually the left – for reading and close work, (Stein 2000). Spectacles are made for the child with the left lens frosted. The child then reads, with their right eye only, for a period of three months.

b)   Coloured Filters

The magnocellular system does not contribute to colour vision but, because it is most sensitive to long wavelengths (red, yellow green) children's eye control can be improved using coloured filters during reading. These are in the form of overlays or coloured lenses. Treatment entails offering the child a choice between five colours; red, yellow, green, blue or a neutral grey density and uses the filter for a three month period. Details of success obtained using both occlusion and different coloured filters can be found in Stein (2000) & Stein, Riddell and Fowler, (1988).

II   Irlen's Coloured Lenses

Theory

Helen Irlen suggests many children with dyslexia are experiencing a perceptual problem she calls *Scotopic Sensitivity Syndrome* (SSS) due to a neurological dysfunction of a biological origin. For people with SSS the brain seems to have difficulty handling full spectrum light. However, Irlen distinguishes her use of the word 'scotopic' from the use of the word as 'night vision' describing SSS as:

> "– sensitivity to certain wavelengths of light (leading to) a
> perceptual difficulty and distortions, most noticeably when
> an individual tries to read black characters on white paper."
> (Irlen 1991, p1)

SSS has five components and a person with SSS may experience any or all of them:

a)   Light Sensitivity

Individuals with SSS may find artificial light 'too bright', with full fluorescent lighting often the worst. The sensitivity to glare in their environment and on the printed page makes it a battle to keep the eye on the page and to move across the line consistently and effectively.

b)   Inadequate Background Accommodation

This is trouble dealing with high contrasts such as between black and white. High contrast is supposed to be best for reading because it allows the letter shapes to dominate with no interference from the background. Those with SSS have insufficient contrast between the black letters and the white background and the background begins to compete for their attention. The white can even become dominant and the letters lose their distinctiveness. Full stops, commas and the dot on top of 'i' may disappear. Letters such as 'b', 'd' and 'p' can be easily confused. Letters such as 'm', 'u', 'w', 'n' and 'h' become hard to distinguish. Letters such as 'a', 'e', 'o' and 'u' can appear to be the same. Reading for more than a few minutes is practically impossible and can cause intense fatigue and headaches.

c)   Poor Print Resolution

Here letters, numbers and symbols appear to dance, vibrate, pulsate, jiggle, shift, shimmer, move or disappear. These problems depend on print size, spacing, typeface and the quantity per page.

d)   Restricted Span of Recognition

This means there is a difficulty reading groups of letters, notes, numerals, or words at the same time. This is also known as tunnel reading. Readers lack the capability to move from line to line, to copy, to proof-read, to skim or to speed-read. Reading books not broken into columns will be difficult, as will be hyphenated words that begin on one line and continue on the next. The visual imagery necessary for spelling is nonexistent and there might be an over-dependence on spelling phonetically.

e)   Lack of Sustained Attention

Readers with this problem will take frequent breaks or do other activities while they regain the stamina necessary to sustain effort at reading.

These perceptual distortions will appear rapidly on beginning to read, usually within 5-10 minutes. SSS is not an 'all-or-nothing' phenomenon. A continuum occurs with symptoms varying from very slight to very severe, depending on the type, onset, number and intensity of distortions.

SSS and Dyslexia

Irlen does not suggest that SSS is the cause of dyslexia in visual subjects, but that it may be one of the additional problems they face and that those dyslexics who have visual/perceptual problems may be suffering from SSS. This may be in addition to their dyslexia, which she notes may cause them problems in other ways than those found in SSS, such as with memory, coordination, depth perception and discerning right from left. However, she is most concerned that if a dyslexic person has SSS s/he may not be accurately assessed, as SSS requires a different method to detect.

Practice

Irlen believes that if the colour wave lengths that may be involved in causing these perceptual distortions were reduced, the brain could more effectively analyse and process information without interference. When SSS is remedied it is like a layer of the problem being removed. It is sometimes sufficient that this layer will in itself resolve the problems. However, Irlen stresses that this is not true for everyone and that they will still need help, but the help will be more effective if the SSS is addressed. Some children with learning problems will not have SSS. This will be discovered at the assessment and screening stages.

Treatment

A   *Screening*

The screening procedures used for SSS do not duplicate anything currently being used to test for academic problems but are unique to Irlen's programme for SSS detection.

Individuals are first recommended to have a full optometrist or opthalmologist examination to show up any visual problems they might have. Correction of these should be undertaken before screening for SSS. Screening involves obtaining information to determine if SSS is affecting reading and learning. Screening identifies whether the person is scotopic. It also indicates whether the individual is a good candidate for additional treatment, which aspect of the person's reading will have the potential to be improved, and which aspects are probably not improvable. Factors in the diagnosis of SSS include the severity of the symptoms, the demands of the educational system, the maturity and verbal skills of the individual, the number and severity of other reading difficulties and in what ways the individual has learned to compensate. It is therefore recommended that children be screened frequently, and from an early age, as lack of verbal skills and maturity may hamper the diagnostic process. There are three parts to the screening:

a)   Questioning of the reader

b)   Tasks to elicit symptoms of SSS

c)   Use of coloured overlays

a)   Questioning
During the screening process the screener will ask exactly what happens when the child tries to read. Children are asked questions such as:

> "When you start to get frustrated and you want to stop reading, tell me what reading is like."

To this, a child might say, "I start to blink a lot." The questioner then asks what happens to make him/her blink and the child will describe their experience. For example:

> "I blink because the words run together and become unreadable. When I blink, it spaces the words out. Now I have spaces between the letters and words. I'm able to read just so long, and then everything seem to shift and merge together again" (Irlen, 1991, p133).

b)   *Tasks*

Each task focuses on a different set of perceptual symptoms and shows the types of distortions that occur for the person during normal reading. They will highlight the same problems the child experiences during reading, but much more quickly.

For example, the child may be able to read for 15-20 minutes before experiencing distortions, but these distortions will occur almost immediately when s/he does the assessment task. For example, in a task called 'The Cube' candidates are shown an illustration of a cube with a grid design on both planes and asked to count the white spaces along the top and down the side. They are then asked to relate whatever difficulties they encountered. Completion of the task is not as important as the types of difficulty experienced. Irlen found that one person rarely has the same degree of difficulty with every activity in this section, but it is important to find out which tasks do cause them trouble.

c)   *Overlays*

If the questions and exercises indicate the presence of SSS, then part 3 applies. This consists of trying a series of coloured overlays to see which one is most effective at improving reading ability by reducing the visual perceptual symptoms. A wide range of overlays will be tried. The overlays will have the desired effect only on the person who is seeing distortions. An individual will be able, often for the first time, to identify the differences between what s/he experiences and those of a good reader. Each individual will have a different result, depending on what other layers or problems are contributing to their reading or learning problems. Irlen says:

> "By the end of the screening, those with SSS will know which coloured overlay to use. In that way, they'll actually have something in hand that they can take away from the testing situation. They'll each take home the coloured overlay (or combination of coloured overlays) that has proven most helpful. They can use it for a while, independently, to assure themselves that the same type of changes they experienced in the session occur time after time in different environments. They'll watch to see if the changes continue when they read at night, or when they read for 15 or 20 minutes, or when they read in the classroom on a day-to-day-basis." (Irlen, 1991, p141)

During the screening other family members are included in the process. This is to help parents check other children and themselves for SSS and to help them understand the nature of the problem their child is experiencing. The child will also feel supported and comforted by their presence and understanding, and later on if a child tries to avoid using the overlays a parent can encourage them to continue.

B   *Lenses*
Positive results from the screening procedure indicate the individual should go for further diagnostic tests and treatment with *lenses*. Irlen stresses that individuals always have a choice not to proceed beyond the overlay stage. However most people find that the overlays become

cumbersome and lenses have greater versatility. Lenses can help improve depth perception and sports performance, make reading under fluorescent lighting, reading music and taking tests easier, as well as many other situations other than reading. The stage after screening involves determining which colour to make a lens so that it best helps the individual's perception. However, the coloured lenses are not called 'glasses', but *filters,* distinguishing them from eyeglasses, which are worn for purely visual problems.

There are literally hundreds of different colours or combinations of colours, but only one that will be helpful for any one person. To identify this, Irlen developed the use of the *photospectrometer,* which measures the characteristic of each colour, and categorises each filter according to the amount of light each colour transmits. This process is precise, intense and often lengthy and can take two hours or more to determine the right colour for the individual. Interestingly, the colour that works best in the filters differs from the one that works best in that person's overlay. Irlen is not entirely clear on why this is, but believes it may be that reflected light from the page remains unmodified by other environmental light sources whereas, when a person wears coloured filters, all light entering the eye is modified.

C   *Environmental Factors*

In addition to the use of lenses, environmental alterations may be made to make the learning context perceptually easier and more enjoyable. Factors influencing the individual can include peer pressure, increased confidence-boosting by the understanding of behavioural problems, avoidance of bad habits around schoolwork, adjusting lighting/removing fluorescent lights, choice of paper colour, (often grey, beige or recycled non-glare is best; avoiding chalk-boards, the use of coloured highlighters for columns and key points, and adopting the use of other non-gloss materials.

A child's other reading problems will need to be addressed separately. In these cases Irlen recommends a multi-sensory literacy programme as the usual choice, (as described in Chapter 5). Although in some cases remediation of SSS will be sufficient to solve their literacy problems, for others the use of the individual's coloured overlay will work by helping to eliminating perceptual distortions, which then enable them to learn through literacy programmes. Approximately one-third of diagnosed dyslexics will not benefit from SSS treatment. Irlen writes:

> "Their dyslexia has other causes which are not understood;
> their problems are too complex for a clear-cut treatment."
> (1999, p105)

The Irlen Centre website gives full details of the seven UK clinics and self-referral details: www.irlen.com/europe.htm Case studies in support of the lenses are available in Irlen (1999, p107-8) and Viadero (1999).

CHAPTER 4

MOVEMENT PROGRAMMES

There were 3 programmes which utilised physical movement in the study:

Brain-Gym, Primary Reflex Inhibition Programme (PRI) and the DORE/DDAT Method. Although each varies in its theory, they share the importance of integrating the balance organs.

1 Brain Gym

Theory
There are three main elements to the philosophy behind *Brain Gym*:

a) Learning is a whole body/mind occurrence and not purely mental

b) There are many combinations (32) of hand/leg/eye/ear/foot/ brain-hemisphere 'wiring' which give individual children different dominance patterns and therefore different learning needs and strengths

c) The role of stress is perceived as causative. Under stress an individual will 'switch off' some neural pathways and therefore be unable to access full sensory information. This gives rise to learning/functional problems.

a)   The Body/Mind as a Whole
In this theory the body plays an integral part in all our intellectual processes from the earliest movements in the womb right through life. It is our bodily senses that feed the brain environmental information with which to form an understanding of the world and from which to draw when creating new possibilities. Sensations, movements, emotions and brain integrative functions are grounded in the body. Therefore the human qualities we associate in the mind can never exist separately from the body. Consequently, what we know, feel, learn and think is shaped by *how* we know, feel, learn and think. How we do things is in turn dependent on our sensory-motor systems through which all our experience of the world and of ourselves is mediated. And the wider our sensory environment and the greater our freedom to explore it, the more intricate will be the patterns for leaning, thought and creativity.

b)   The 32 Dominance Profiles
In *Brain Gym* there are 32 possible different Dominance Profiles which cover all the possible combinations of eye, ear, hand, foot and brain 'wiring'. These are considered to be innate or basal differences and are important if children are to be both understood and their strengths and weaknesses appreciated. Paul Dennison, the originator of *Brain Gym*, found in studies of the eyes during thought processes that right and left-brained people exist in equal numbers, no matter which hand and eye are apparently dominant. Consequently, *Brain Gym* uses the concept of 'brained-ness' rather than 'handedness' to define dominance:

"Those right-handed, right-eyed people who feel frustrated and inhibited in learning may be right-brained without knowing it, although appearing to be left-brained." (Dennison, 1981, p61)

c) The Role of Stress in Dyslexia

It is thought here that the brain functions best when operating as an integrated whole, able to process all sensory input and interact with the environment. However, when the person is under stress they may 'switch off' and no longer function in an integrated manner which can cause problems. Consequently it is thought:

> "The dyslexic, whether through brain trauma, congenital birth defect, emotional stress, or hyperactivity, does not integrate right brain and left brain automatically when dealing with symbols." (Dennison, 1981, p36)

There are a variety of sources of 'stress' given in this model, but these usually incur an over-activation of the 'fight or flight' or survival mechanism of the body.

The flight/fight response is a correct response to actual danger, but in prolonged or on-going stress 'switching off' constrains the child's brain activity to the top of the brain stem thus effectively keeping them in 'survival mode'. Perpetually responding to stress with survival-based behaviour negatively affects the nervous system.

Anything the child perceives as a threat rather than a learning opportunity may subsequently become an on-going source of stress. Hannaford believes:

> "People who live with a great deal of stress may inadequately develop the neural pathways that form the foundations for new learning, reasoning and creativity." (Hannaford, 1995, p64)

However, if we choose to perceive events as learning, or an adventure, neurotransmitters like GABA, acetylcholine, interferon and interlukins are released. These increase our ability to establish or reorganise neural networks so we may effectively think and remember.

Stress can be communicated to babies and children from very early on, even before birth. They may be affected by their mother's high adrenalin levels or sense the fears and tensions around them and become stressed themselves. In particular boys may suffer because they are two-three weeks behind girls in their development at birth. Infants who exhibit elevated adrenalin levels are also more vulnerable to chronic ear infections. Frank and Harold Levinson's found that 94-97% of children with learning difficulties showed two or more abnormal electronystagmographic (ENG) parameters indicating a cerebellar/vestibular (balance) system dysfunction. All of these children had experienced trauma to this area through ear infections, allergies or being shaken as infants (Levinson, 1988).

The Vestibular System

The vestibular system is the first sensory system to fully develop. It is visible in a two-month old embryo and is fully developed and myelinated by 5 months after conception. The vestibular system has great significance in *Brain Gym*. Whereas it is usual to consider only the five senses that carry information from the body; sight, audition, smell, taste and touch, in this theory the integration of information about the body from gravity and motion in space is considered vital in developing an ability to understand and learn. The organs of the vestibular system are considered in this model to be the most sensitive of all sense organs. The vestibular system maintains both static and dynamic equilibrium. Static equilibrium refers to the orientation of the body, mainly the head, relative to gravity. Dynamic equilibrium maintains the body's position in response to sudden movements such as acceleration, deceleration and rotation when in motion. About 20% of the messages from the eyes, from the retina and extra-ocular muscles, go to areas of the brain concerned with balance.

In a car, plane or boat, a sense of dis-equilibrium can sometimes result as the system works hard to maintain a still head in a moving body, with the constant change of gravity, acceleration and deceleration. When no resolution of the two is possible the body will usually vomit in order to release the eye movements.

Movement

The vestibular nuclei carries impulses from the semicircular canals of the ears and from the cerebellum, to the Reticular Activating System (RAS) in the brain stem.

The RAS 'wakes up' the cortex of the brain increasing excitability and responsiveness to incoming stimuli from the environment. This 'wake up' prepares us to take in and respond to our surroundings and to learn. When we don't move and activate the vestibular system we are not taking in information from the environment. Hence, *Brain Gym* perceives movement as the natural learning path. From conception onwards the child gains a sense of gravity and knowledge of the physical environment through movement.

> "Beginning with only reflexive movement at birth, the child
> learns to stand, walk and even run in a gravitational field by
> approximately one year old." (Hannaford, 1995, p36)

Each movement stimulates the vestibular system, which stimulates the brain for new learning. Movement is thus essential to learning as it awakens and activates many of our mental capacities as well as integrating the body with the mind and anchoring new information and experience into neural networks. Because of the emphasis on body/mind development and the importance of movement, it is considered premature within *Brain Gym* to attempt to teach a child to read before about 7 years of age unless they freely choose to sit and look at books without pressure and expectation.

Proprioception and Touch

Proprioception is the sensation from muscles, tendons and the vestibular system that together enable the brain to determine the position of the body in space. It is mediated through receptors in the skin. Skin is therefore one of the primary organs for early environmental learning. All sensations travel through the brain stem to the thalamus and then to the somatosensory area of the cortex, (the parietal lobe). The frontal eye field coordinates eye movements, allowing tracking and integration of line and shaping three-dimensionality. When the balanced activation of this system is interfered with we become 'uncentred' and disorientated, losing our balance and our physical sense of ourselves. Touch after birth stimulates growth of the body's sensory nerve endings involved in motor movements, orientation and visual perception.

If these nerve endings are not activated, the RAS that awakens the brain cortex will not operate fully. This leads to impaired muscular movements, curtailed sensory intake and a variety of emotional disturbances and learning defects.

Bilateral Functioning – 'Switching-On'

Brain Gym considers cross crawling to be the initial way in which the child develops integrated brain-hemisphere function. The first form of crawling is usually homo-lateral where the limbs on the same side of the body move together as a reflex. The infant may lie on his back and move his limbs simultaneously or crawl on her tummy with her head on the floor so that only one eye can see at one time.

This is then replaced with cross crawling as the infant learns to integrate cross-motor patterns. In this theory it is suggested that most dyslexics have not learned to internalise cross-motor patterning and therefore have difficulty when returning to it in reading and writing where the same bilateral integration is required:

> "In order to read, to write, to spell, to listen, or to be integrated for any activity, for that matter, one must be able to 'cross the midline' which connects right and left brain, the two opposing polarities of the body. The midline is either a bridge or a barrier to learning, depending upon polarity imbalances within one's system." (P&G Dennison, 1985, p11)

Cross-lateral movements activate both hemispheres in a balanced way thus 'switching-on' whole-brain activities. These activities work both sides of the body evenly and involve coordinated movements of both eyes, both ears, both hands and both feet, as well as balanced core muscles. By this method the corpus callosum, connecting the two hemispheres of the brain, which is responsible for orchestrating processes between them, becomes fully developed. In dyslexia, where stress has 'switched off' whole-brain integration, cross-motor patterning is perceived to be a key exercise in restoring whole-brain function and therefore 'switching-on' full sensory processing.

However, Dennison found that cross-crawling techniques such as 'patterning,' devised by Dolman and Delacato, which attempt to replicate cross-crawling often didn't work with dyslexics. He believes this is because they have moved beyond the stage where they had become conscious of self. In babyhood, when cross crawling begins, this is not yet achieved and the baby is largely right-hemisphere orientated and un-self-conscious. Later, when the left hemisphere has become more involved, the activity of cross crawling appears to worsen the problem. Dennison therefore devised a corrective version of this method, which he called *Dennison Laterality Repatterning*. This forms the basis of further exercises which are now known as the *Brain Gym* programme, all of which are designed to enable integrated, whole brain activity.

Practice

A   Assessment

The first step is to establish the child's *Dominance Profile*. This takes the form of a simple step-by-step assessment, which can be done by anyone with a helper. (Hannaford, 1997, p38-9 gives full details). The information gained means the child's profile can be found from the 32 variations. A *DomiKnow Chart* is used to fill in the profile of the individual, showing their hand, eye, ear, foot and brain-hemisphere preference. When the individual's dominance profile has been found it is possible to see their learning strengths and weaknesses. This concept is also known in other educational practice as a child's *Learning Style*.

B   Treatment

There are two stages to this:

a)   Each of the 32 different profiles has accompanying *Helps*, which indicate ways of teaching the child, aimed specifically at their individual dominance pattern.

b)   The aim of becoming more whole-brained and/or integrated is met largely by a variety of cross-lateral physical movements which together comprise *Brain Gym*. These are put together in a programme lasting about 15 minutes to be done by an individual every day at home, or sometimes before learning activities in school as a whole-class exercise.

Support for *Brain Gym* can be found in Freeman (2000), EKF Research Study Summaries (2003) and Paul Dennison (1981). Full details of the 32 dominance profiles, the *Helps* for each, and many *Brain Gym* exercises are given in Hannaford (1997). Further information is available at: www.braingym.org

II   Primary Reflex Inhibition Programme (PRI)

Theory
Here, not all, but many cases of dyslexia are thought to be the result of retained primary reflexes. These reflexes are present in unborn babies and are gradually replaced by secondary, postural reflexes as the child develops. Primary reflexes are a core part of the architecture of the central nervous system (CNS). They are consequently never lost but by 18 months most have inhibited or transformed into different movements. However, problems can occur if the primary reflexes fail to inhibit. Through the observation of hundreds of unborn babies at the Foetal Behaviour Research Centre, Royal Maternity Hospital, Belfast, Martin McPhillips and his team established that the unborn baby makes all the classic reflex patterns. However, movements are more stereotyped than those of newborn babies. McPhillips describes primary reflexes as equivalent to 'the caterpillar stage in humans' before the postural reflex system takes over at about one year of age.

This is at the time when we move from a prone to upright stance. Full orientation in a gravitational environment therefore depends on moving through the primary to the secondary reflex systems.

"People develop a kind of three dimensional grid, that they operate within. If you take gravity out of the grid, then ordering becomes more difficult – everything starts to shift. This is the trouble faced by dyslexic children, because as long as the primary system is there it won't allow you to develop the grid system." (Smyth, 2001, p83)

As they develop, postural reflexes inhibit primary reflexes through basic movement patterns. And, it appears that the more the baby performs the reflex pattern the greater the likelihood it will switch off the primary reflex and enable further development. Uninhibited reflexes, which remain active beyond the optimum time, will therefore interfere with this process. A number of possible causations for retained reflexes are suggested, such as excess toxins or adrenaline present in the womb during development; the manner of birth; vaccination effects or illness.

Movement and Learning
Reflex movements provide a child with its earliest movement vocabulary. Movement feeds information to the brain, helping to develop a sense of the body map and spatial awareness in the interaction between the self and environment. The cerebellum utilises this information to modify and refine subsequent motor activity. Learning takes place in the brain but it is the body that acts as the receptor for information and then becomes the vehicle through which knowledge is expressed. Because all children do not develop at the same pace, some may enter formal school at a disadvantage. For example, when tested, McPhillips found dyslexic boys three times more likely to have persistent primary reflexes than girls and to have a generally weaker Central Nervous System (CNS). Their neurological development was not sufficient for the tasks they were expected to undertake. He says:

"There is a basic assumption that all children commencing school start with the same ability to perform these tasks. Therefore when children fail, the school or the teachers are used as scapegoats – or blame is pointed at the child's home." (Smyth, 2001, p83)

The refined motor skills children are expected to perform, such as holding a pencil, or following words on a page, are simply beyond the developmental capability of some children at that point. This is despite adequate intellectual ability. The overall effect is described by Goddard, co-director of the INPP reflex inhibition programme:

"It is as if later skills remain tethered to an earlier stage of development, and instead of becoming automatic can only be mastered through continuous conscious effort." (Goddard, 2002, p2)

Whist there are many primitive reflexes, which all play important roles in the gradual maturation of the child, two in particular, the *Tonic Labyrinthine Reflex* (TLR) and *Asymmetrical Tonic Neck Reflex* (ATNR) appear particularly connected with dyslexia.

The Tonic Labyrinthine Reflex (TLR)

The TLR is vestibular in origin and is elicited by movement of the body and/or head and alteration of position in space. The TLR reflex ensures that lowering of the baby's head below the level of the spine will cause immediate extension of the arms and legs. The TLR in extension reflex is thought to emerge as the baby's head enters the birth canal and should be fully present from the time of birth. Inhibition of the TLR as the head falls forwards is accomplished by c. 4 months of age. Inhibition of the TLR on the head falling backwards is more gradual, involving the emergence of several postural reflexes, and taking up to age 3 to be complete. By 6 months of age the development of head-control modifies the response. Head control is an essential prerequisite for the development of all later functions. The TLR exerts a tonic influence upon the distribution of muscle tone throughout the body, literally helping the infant to 'straighten out' from the flexed position of the foetus and the newborn. Thus balance, muscle tone and proprioception are all trained during this process.

Retained TLR

If the TLR fails to inhibit at the correct time it will constantly 'trip' the vestibular in its actions and in its interactions with other sensory systems. The child who has a retained TLR when he starts to walk will experience difficulty in judging space, distance, depth and speed. Sense of direction, up from down, left from right and back from front may also be erratic. If head control is lacking, eye functioning will also be impaired as the eyes operate from the same circuit in the brain – the vestibulo-occular arc. If one segment of the circuit is malfunctioning it will affect the smooth operation of other systems dependent upon that circuit. Balance will be affected by faulty visual information and vision will be affected by poor balance.

The retained TLR may also prevent the child from being able to creep/crawl on his hands and knees as movement of the head back or forward below the level of the spine will result in the automatic reflex extension of the legs.

The Asymmetrical Tonic Neck Reflex (ATNR)

A second major reflex often found in children with dyslexia is the ATNR. This facilitates movement (the kick), develops muscle tone and provides vestibular stimulation. It is believed this reflex should be fully established by the time the baby is ready to be born, so that it may participate in the birth process. Labour should not begin until the unborn baby has reached maturity, at which time the baby releases the hormone which will stimulate contractions of the mother's uterus. Mother and baby may then act as cooperative partners in the birth process. As the second stage of labour is achieved the baby should help to 'unscrew' itself down the birth canal in rhythm with the mother's contractions. The baby's active partnership in this is dependent upon the presence of a full ATNR. The birth process itself reinforces the ATNR (and other reflexes) so that they are firmly established and active during the first months of life. It enables the baby to turn its head to one side to allow free passage of air when in the prone position and prevents the baby from lying face down when on its tummy. It helps increase extensor muscle tone, trains one side of the body at a time, and provides the basis for later reaching movements. The ATNR is present at the time that visual-fixation upon nearby objects is developing and when the nervous system ensures the appropriate arm stretches out towards visualised objects and the seeds of an awareness of distance (arm's length) and eye-hand coordination are sown. By 6 months of age the ATNR should have completed its task and the developing brain should release further movement patterns, which contain the inhibitor to the ATNR, allowing more complex skills to be acquired.

Retained ATNR
This was found to be present in many dyslexic children. Continued presence of the ATNR will interfere with numerous functions:

• Balance may be affected as result of hand movements to either side

• Homolateral, rather than cross-lateral movements, eg when walking, marching, skipping, etc

• Difficulty crossing the midline

- Poor 'ocular pursuit', especially when visually crossing the midline

- Mixed laterality. (Child may use left foot, right hand, left ear, or he may use left or right hand interchangeably for the same task)

- Poor handwriting and poor expression of ideas on paper

- Visual-perceptual difficulties, particularly in symmetrical representation of figures

The presence of the ATNR is also thought to be a reliable indicator of total reflex persistence (delayed maturation of all other reflexes.)

Reflexes and the Vestibular

Vestibular and reflex systems are inter-dependent in the control of posture and movement. Vestibular dysfunction can alter the level of reflex response, and reflex abnormalities can impede the functioning of the vestibular system. Inappropriate vestibular signals may elicit primitive reflex reactions, but equally, aberrant reflex activity will impede the activities of the vestibular system. If a child is to utilise the information provided by his senses there must be a balance between these systems.

Touch

Our first source of contact with the outside world is through touch. Approximately 5 weeks after conception a response to tactility can be noticed in the unborn child. The grasping reflexes (palmer, plantar, rooting, sucking, Moro, etc.) emerge during the second and third trimester of pregnancy, so that by birth the baby associates touch with security, feeding, comfort and eventually exploration:

"Touch precedes both hearing and vision as the primary channel of learning. - Touch receptors cover the whole body." (Goddard, 2002, p60)

Goddard (2002) also cites Schore who states:

"Most of a child's early touch experiences are provided by the mother during feeding, changing and play. – She acts as the primary facilitator in the early months for the formation of connections between different levels in the brain and the laying of foundations not only for later learning ability but also for emotional functioning and immune response." (p136);

And Diamond and her colleagues, (1963) describe the mother as:

"– playing the role of higher brain structures (to the child). She is the child's auxiliary cortex." (Goddard, 2002, p136, note 6)

Practice

A reflex stimulation/inhibition program acts through a neurological feedback mechanism to inhibit those reflexes which have been retained and are therefore interfering with the child's development. This enables the child to 'catch-up' with their physical development and improve cerebellar functioning by maturing the postural reflex system through which the cerebellum operates. Inhibition of a reflex in infancy frequently correlates with the acquisition of a new skill; so reflex chronology and knowledge of child development are here combined to indicate which aberrant reflex is actively hindering later skills in the older child. This information, obtained through assessment of each reflex, enables the treatment programme to be targeted for the individual child.

A   Assessment

The presence of persistent primary reflexes may be determined in a number of ways. Each side of the body is scored separately and then a total obtained for both sides. (Full details for each reflex are given in Goddard, 2002).

B   Treatment

Remediation involves replicating the movements that would normally effect the inhibition of the reflex involved through physical stimulation and/or exercises.

For example, in McPhillips' remediation programme the children were given slow, stereotypical movements to perform, which replicated the primary reflexes found in much younger infants. This specific sequence of movements was performed daily at home for 10 minutes each evening. Each child was seen at 2 monthly intervals and the sequence of movements changed or adapted. The entire treatment programme lasted 12 months. Other practitioners have developed individual programmes for the child based on their assessments. A boy of 15, for example, diagnosed as profoundly dyslexic, was treated for one month by 20 minutes per day stroking the fingers across his face. In the second month this altered to brushing down from the base of his nose, around the mouth to his chin and then across the top lip. This mimics the reflex patterns of the baby in the womb by touch, rather than after birth. Treatment is usually carried out at the child's home by their parents or an adult friend.

More details of successful studies can be found in McPhillips (2001); McPhillips, Hepper and Mulhern (2000) and at the INPP website: www.INPP.org.uk

Martin McPhillips can be contacted at: m.mcphillips@qub.ac.uk

III   Dore/DDAT Exercise Programme

Theory

This programme was developed by Wynford Dore who describes dyslexia as one form of an under-active cerebellum, suggesting:

> "–all of these symptoms (dyslexia) are the result of a medical condition known as Cerebellar Developmental Delay or CDD. The cerebellum is under-developed and therefore is not able to process the information going to and from the thinking brain quickly enough" (Dore Achievement Centre website, 2004)

CDD

Half the cells in the body, memory and emotions are concentrated in the cerebellum and it has a great many connections to the cortex, or 'thinking brain,' The cortex, the part of the brain responsible for intelligence, is usually quite healthy in dyslexic people, many of whom have above average intelligence. But if the neural pathways, which link the cortex and cerebellum are not yet fully developed, the cerebellum cannot process information quickly enough. This is called cerebellar developmental delay, or CDD. Dore believes one in 6 people have symptoms of CDD, yet most go undiagnosed.

Balance and the Cerebellum

Three factors bring about balance: the somatosensory feelings (what is felt through muscles and joints); vestibular information (from the inner ear balance organ) and visual sensory data from the eyes. The cerebellum is responsible for analysing and co-ordinating all sensory information, and for the co-ordination and balance of the body. Dore refers to the work cited in Chapter 1 (Nicolson & Fawcett, 1999) on the cerebellum in suggesting a link between dyslexia and co-ordinating movement and his programme is largely based upon this. Therefore, under-development of the cerebellum is believed to create dyslexic symptoms as one aspect of CDD together with dyspraxia and/or attention difficulties, which are often present in dyslexic people in addition to their reading and writing problems.

The Cerebellum and Learning

Research has shown the cerebellum is highly active during learning processes, becoming much less so once a skill becomes automatic. When learning how to perform a task an individual will think about the sequence of events and then what needs to be completed within each step. Through practice and repetition they will then be able to perform the task almost without thinking, gaining automaticity. For persons with learning difficulties, automaticity is not achieved for many skills. Simple skills such as reading, writing, and spelling consequently remain very difficult.

Brain Plasticity

Dore's programme is built on the 'plastic' capacity of the brain to build new neural networks through stimulation – here represented by physical activity. The exercises stimulate the cerebellum to create new neural pathways which speed up the processing of information and, in doing so, help with learning, language, emotion and motor skills. Furthermore, this is said to be a permanent improvement, which completely removes the dyslexic symptoms.

Practice

The DORE Programme uses repetitive, co-ordination and balancing activities to develop the capacity for automaticity by enabling the cerebellum to mature. The exercises comprise a variety of cross lateral, throwing, marching, balancing and juggling activities. There are two stages: an initial assessment followed by an individualised exercise plan.

A   *Assessment*

The initial assessment lasts 3-4 hours and includes a doctor's appointment to undertake a medical history and tests to reveal if there are other reasons for learning or reading difficulties. A basic neurological assessment will help eliminate these and therefore prevent inappropriate treatment. The doctor provides a full report of the results of tests and makes appropriate recommendations on therapy.

The Tests

There are several of these:

1   Posturography – this includes a) sensory organisation analysis; b) centre of gravity variation and c) adaption response

The posturography machine was developed by NASA to measure disorientation in astronauts after space flights. It is used to measure the ability to balance under varying conditions. The individual is required only to stand on its platform and stare forward. S/he wears a harness for safety purposes while the base moves. A sensory organisation analysis is made to assess the appropriate use of sensory information for the control of posture. Centre of gravity variation and strategies used to balance are also measured by the sensory-organisation test. Muscular disturbance of balance is measured through the motor-control test as the person adjusts to forward/backward motion. The adaption-test measures how an individual adapts to various changes of posture in which the cerebellum has to over-ride normal reactions, thus showing how well sensory information is being processed.

2   Eye movements are assessed in co-ordination with moving target lights. Several types are measured: a) smooth pursuit; b) saccadic; c) optokinetic and d) gaze.

3   The Dyslexia Screening Test (DST) developed by Nicholson and Fawcett (1996) is used to establish the severity of the individual's dyslexic symptoms.

B   *Treatment*
The patient is given an individualised programme of movements drawn from a range of dozens of different ones. The exercise programme will take a total of approximately 10 minutes to perform twice per day.

Exercises
The programme is made up to suit the individual child from hundreds of different physical exercises. These include:

• Running round an object while looking up

• Throwing a bean-bag under the leg and catching it with the opposite hand

• Marching/walking cross-laterally on the spot

• Balancing on a wobble board

• Standing on one leg while throwing a beanbag from one hand to the other.

• Walking downstairs backwards

• Juggling with bean bags

Interim Progress Assessment

On average six progress assessments are also made. These take place on average every 6 weeks throughout the course of treatment. At each assessment the patient is retested and a new exercise programme created as appropriate. This takes about 1-1.5 hours

Final Assessment

The individual is assessed again for physiological progress by the doctor and given posturography, eye-movement and dyslexia re-tests. The final assessment, doctor's consultation and report take about 3 hours. The programme varies in length between 9-12 months. It is recommended that before commencing the programme any essential fatty acids or oral hay fever (antihistamine) drugs are suspended for the duration of the course.

A School's study with the DORE programme has been undertaken by Reynolds, Nicolson and Hambly (2003) with follow-up support in Nicolson (2003). Case studies can be found at Berliner (2003) and on the Dore/DDAT website: www.ddat.org

CHAPTER 5

MULTISENSORY PROGRAMMES

There were 3 different multisensory programmes in the study: *Alpha-to-Omega* literacy programme, the Ron Davis Method and Music-Making.

I   *Alpha-to-Omega*

Theory

By the time they commence literacy most children have refined sound-awareness of the links made by 'mapping' sounds to speech and the actions surrounding them. However, dyslexic children are thought to have weak internal sound representations. It is believed that this 'fuzzy' mapping can be improved by a form of teaching which emphasises *simultaneous stimulation* through the use of the four senses involved: visual, auditory, visual-kinaesthetic and oral-kinaesthetic. These refer to the seen, heard, seen-when-felt, (such as a solid letter shape) and felt-when spoken, (the feel of the tongue in mouth when the letter/sound is spoken) aspects. Reading and writing are themselves multisensory activities. Multisensory methods rely on re-connecting these different sense associations:

"–remedying the phonological weaknesses of children with

these specific difficulties by the systematic building up of associations between speech, sounds and their representation in writing. (Miles & Miles, 1990, p88)

Although there were earlier multisensory approaches, *Alpha to Omega* (Hornsby & Shear, 1975) was the first structured phonic/linguistic system for dyslexics in the UK.

It adopts a logical structure of language, following what would occur with a young child and beginning, 'as does the infant,' with phonological acquisition.

The 'telegrammatic' speech of the infant is likened to the leaving out of the 'little' words in the dyslexic's written work. A strict order to the teaching of consonants is stressed, finishing with consonant blends, which are usually problematic and require much discrimination. Of the vowels, only their names and their short sounds are taught to begin with and the rest introduced gradually. Content words – nouns, verbs and adjectives are taught first – while function words – the 'little' words; prepositions, particles, etc. – come last.

Practice

There are two processes involved in this programme: reading and writing.

A   Reading

For reading – translation from written symbol to sound – the method uses the standard *Alpha to Omega Flashcards*, available as a ready-made set with the following instructions:

1.   The teacher presents the letter on a flashcard with the key picture drawn on the reverse side. The pupil should say the letter's name

2.   The teacher says the key word and then the sound of the letter

3.   The pupil repeats the key word and sound

4.   The teacher says the sound and then the name

5.   The pupil repeats the sound and gives the name, writing it as he says it (translating the sound he has heard into written letters)

6.   The pupil reads what he has written, giving the sound (translating the letters written into sounds that are heard)

7.   The pupil writes the letter with the eyes closed to get the feel of the letter (When vision is cut off, other senses, such as touch are sharpened)

When the child is reasonably familiar with the names, sounds and shapes of the letters this drill can be modified.

Following this, the five basic vowel sounds are taught, including the semi-vowel 'y'. Next, the remaining nineteen vowel sounds are gradually revealed plus the other twenty-five consonant sounds. This involves the concept of 'chunking' of certain combinations. Then come consonant blends, vowel/consonant 'chunks' and modification of sounds by other letters. Gradually the complete range of spelling patterns is covered, culminating in the final syllables 'tion', 'cian', 'tial', 'cious', 'cient', etc. From here the pupil progresses to sentences. The authors stress simple, active, affirmative, declarative (SAAD) sentences such as:

The man ran to the red van
A black cat jumped onto the table

Overall, the course falls into three stages:

Stage One uses games, proof-reading exercises, rhymes, dictation of sentences and visual associations to teach letters, vowels, blends, digraphs and varied meanings of the same words and transformations, autonyms and synonyms, in addition to comprehension and story writing. Additional games and teaching aids are available from the authors to back up the course. At the end of Stage One a marking scheme is given to enable progress to be measured. If necessary, parts of the stage are re-done or the child may progress more quickly if progress is good.

Stage Two covers vowel digraphs, confusable words, the possessive apostrophe, abbreviations for information, homophones, how to use a dictionary, letter writing, expressive writing, English structure, writing a business letter, the passive, composition, précis, comprehension and punctuation. Also suffixing part 1, dialogue and reported speech, and plurals. A combination of games, exercises, sentences for dictation, proof-reading, rhymes to write, words to read visually and anagrams is used. There is a spelling test at the end of Stage Two to assess whether the child is ready to move to Stage Three or requires revision of previous stage material before moving on.

Stage Three uses words of more than one syllable for the first time with exercises emphasising the divisions for stress marking, final syllables, analogies, suffixing part 2, advanced passives, advanced reported speech, writing plays, formal and informal registers, the conditional and cause and effect ('if/should') proverbs, more homophones, silent letters, countries, surnames, Greek and Latin prefixes/suffixes, hints on essay writing and exams, reading for different purposes and a conclusion, giving a rough guide to spelling ages for each of the three stages.

B   Handwriting

The need to help dyslexic children break up the word-strings they hear into separate words are stressed. It is believed the child with dyslexia can only learn to do this by writing practice – translation from sound to letter – which must also be taught in the same clear, logical approach. Lower case *Manuscript* is used. Hornsby and Shear recommend beginning with writing capitals as these use circles and lines which all children can draw, and are therefore sympathetic to the developmental capabilities of the child and easier to reproduce. However, they dislike 'ball and stick' writing, and Hornsby favours a modified cursive style as a fully cursive style causes later difficulties when letters do not always start at the base line. The use of a medium-soft pencil initially is recommended rather than a pen. Corrections can then be erased neatly. A fountain pen is better than a ballpoint as it must be held correctly in order to work. The correct grip and posture are encouraged from the start. Left-handers are recommended left-handed nibs. Advice on the angle of the pen and grip are also given. Tracing of the letters is the first stage until these are committed to memory.

Grammatical structure is taught in the following order:

> Parts of speech, punctuation, tense, personal pronoun replacement, possessive pronoun replacement, relative pronoun replacement, "wh" words, shortened forms, dialogue, reported speech, different registers – informal, formal, summaries, note taking, essay writing, writing learned papers.

Sentences

In writing sentences the following procedure is followed:

1.   Dictate the whole sentence, as you would normally say it

2.   Ask the pupil to repeat it aloud

3.   Dictate it again, isolating each word and speaking very
      clearly so that he does not hear the words run together in
      strings, but separately, as they will be written down (making
      the translation from spoken to written language)

4.   The pupil writes the sentence, saying it clearly as he writes it
      (he is now making the translation from spoken to written
      language for himself)

5.   Ask pupil to read aloud exactly what he has written

6.   Suggest final corrections if the pupil fails to discover them
      for himself

The method used above increases the child's memory for sentences, as
shorter ones give way to longer. Once the dyslexic pupil has mastered
SAAD sentences they can progress to more sophisticated structures.
This process therefore parallels the way a baby develops language
(Hornsby, 1984). The Beve Hornsby website gives full details of this
programme, research and educational courses: www.hornsby.co.uk/

II   Ron Davis Method

Theory
Dyslexia is here perceived as a talent or 'gift' rather than a brain
'malfunction', which comes about because of the ostensibly visual
mentality of dyslexic people. This can create a peculiar disorientation in
situations such as reading or writing, where no meaningful visual image
can be formed in the 'mind's eye'. The resulting disorientation is seen as
the symptoms of dyslexia.

Visual-Spatial Thinking

Ron Davis perceives people with dyslexia as right-hemisphere 'systems thinkers' who need to see the contextual meaning of the information before they can understand the parts. They can be excellent at mathematical analysis but make many computational errors, for example. Traditional education is not designed for these thinkers as concepts are traditionally introduced in step-by-step fashion, practised with drill and repetition, assessed under timed conditions and then reviewed. This process is ideal for sequential learners, (usually left-brain hemisphere dominant) who progress step-by-step from easy to difficult, but does not suit the mind that needs to see the meaningful whole before the parts. For dyslexic children concepts are quickly comprehended when they are presented within a context and related to other concepts. Once spatial learners can create a mental picture of a concept and see how the information fits with what they already know their learning is permanent. Repetition is completely unnecessary and irrelevant to their learning style.

Disorientation

"Orientation means knowing where you are in relation to your environment. In terms of perception, it means finding out the facts and conditions of your surroundings and putting yourself in the proper relation to them." (Davis, 1997, p15)

Although this non-verbal conceptualisation is a 'gift,' Davis suggests it can become a liability in situations where a dyslexic person comes across a word that cannot be so pictured and they experience a contextual, perceptual disorientation. Any abstract word for which they cannot form an image will trigger this 'disorientation'. (Davis has highlighted 217 'trigger words', although each child will have their own variations). Davis believes:

"All of the symptoms of dyslexia are symptoms of

disorientation. – Common examples of disorientation include motion sickness, the sense of falling when on an escalator or at the edge of a cliff, 'hearing things' and the false sense of motion people sometimes experience when they are sitting in a stationary vehicle and see another nearby vehicle move. (Davis, 1997, p125-6)

Practice

There are three main stages. Full details of each of the following elements are in Davis, 1997 *Assessment, Orientation Counselling* and *Symbol Mastery.*

A   Assessment

The Perceptual Ability Assessment shows if the person is a candidate for the programme. It involves the child making a mental image of an object (usually a piece of chocolate cake) with eyes closed and mentally looking at it from different view- points. Then the child is asked to place their 'minds eye' in their finger tip and the finger is then moved by the practitioner to different positions, while the child is asked to move their 'mind's eye with their finger and look at the object from there. Then the child is asked to put their 'mind's eye' back to the original view. This procedure will highlight any cognitive 'off-centred' visual perception (disorientation) and also the child's ability to visualise.

B   Orientation Counselling

This is again a mental activity which will balance the child's perceptual ability whenever disorientation occurs. The child's handedness is established and the aim of orientation counselling explained to the child as: putting yourself in the proper position in relation to the facts of your surroundings'. Using the minds eye and mental imagery, with eyes closed, the child is asked to picture an object and to anchor it in the optimum orientation point. There is only one orientation point where all sensory data are most accurate. 'The point' is c.30cm above and slightly behind the head. 'Anchor lines' are visualised holding the object in place, which the child draws in the mind. The mental object can then be moved to the optimum 'point' easily. When the child has been taught how to 'return to point' any off-centred mental perceptions, he/she will be able to orientate him/herself if/whenever disorientation is triggered. It usually takes less than an hour to go through this procedure with the child.

C   *Basic Symbol Mastery*

After Orientation Counselling, *Symbol Mastery* is used to create a meaningful visual image from clay for all the triggers of disorientation. For the dyslexic, a word has three parts: what it means, what it looks like and what it sounds like. The clay models made in symbol mastery are for the *word meaning* in picture form. Each clay figure utilises a multisensory approach to give meaning to the look, sound, spoken experience and feel of the word to the child. Letters and symbols are also made in clay. Fig 8 below shows a clay model representing a child's trigger 'over':

Fig 8. 'A child's representation of 'over' in clay.
Photo. Courtesy of Hilary Farmer, *Davis Dyslexia Practitioner.*

The child creates each symbol as they wish, and only as they wish, in modelling clay, identifies it, touching it while speaking its name and learns its use. For the alphabet each letter is created starting with the upper case and working from A-Z. To correct the learning disability of dyslexia all the trigger words and symbols must be learned and mastered. These exercises are done individually with the child at their own pace. Breaks are taken often, especially after a success. The work with the alphabet is complete when a child can recite the alphabet forwards and backwards with equal ease and speed and can tell what letters come before and after every other letter in the alphabet. Over a period of several months the entire list of small words is mastered, two to three definitions at a time. Punctuation marks are made in the same way. Because words are symbols that represent both sound and meaning, it is important that the student also be coached through all the speech sounds. This doesn't require a speech therapist, only the pronunciation key from any dictionary and a good coach. If numbers 'trigger' disorientation for the child, the same basic process is done with these.

Reading
Davis suggests three ways to help dyslexics with learning to read.

1.   Spell Reading
This trains the student in left to right eye movement in reading. This is not phonics or a phonetic process; it is simply letter and word recognition.

2.   Sweep-Sweep-Spell
The purpose of this exercise is to continue training in left-right eye movement and word recognition. Understanding what is read is not yet the goal. The instruction is:

"Let your eyes sweep through (or over) the word. If the

word doesn't just come out of your mouth, sweep it again. If it doesn't come out of your mouth the second time, spell it. Then I'll tell you what it is and you repeat it."

3.   *Picture-At-Punctuation*

The goal of *Picture-at-Punctuation* is full and complete comprehension of what is read.

"We are now going to add meaning to what you're reading. To us, punctuation means, 'picture'. When you see a punctuation mark, make a picture in your mind of what you have just read."

The Ron Davis programme is not usually recommended for children who have not yet commenced literacy because until they do the child has not yet experienced the disorientation that is dyslexia. The Davis website has many case studies as well as quantitative research conducted with this programme: www.dyslexia.com.

Davis (1997) is a guide for parents/adults on how to use the method.

III   Music-Making

Theory
In this model there is an acceptance of music making as sharing with literacy methods the effect of the simultaneous application of multiple senses. Douglas and Willatts (1994) cite Wisby (1980) who proposed that reading difficulties could be prevented by using musical activities to help children develop a multisensory awareness and response to sounds. Music making can therefore serve the same purpose as multisensory literacy phonics programmes, except it is:

"– 'non-threatening' and 'accepted as something to enjoy'
(Douglas & Johnson, 1995, p88)

In fact, *The Campaign for Music in the Curriculum* states that learning music has been found:

"– to improve reading ability, maths, science and engineering, speech fluency and foreign languages, social skills, memorising capacity, reasoning capacity, time management skills, learning ability, problem solving ability and ability to handle stress. –The case for music is overwhelming." (CMC, 1998)

Music and the Brain

When children study music or learn to play an instrument there are general benefits to their cognitive development. The reason for this is not exactly understood, but it is theorised that music is a multiple sensory process, having physical, emotional and cognitive effects. It utilises both hemispheres of the brain in harmony, thus creating whole-brain activity. Douglas and Johnston (1995) suggest there are many similarities between music and reading: both have written words and symbol systems; and there is the need to decipher written symbols and relate them to the sounds they represent.

As children progress with music they learn to group symbols and this is the same as 'chunking' and word formation. One cortical area of particular importance receives all of the sensory input from the sensory modalities, as well as directly from the thalamus in the limbic system and the reticular activating system (RAS) in the brainstem. This is the inferior parietal lobe (IPL) which integrates information from all sensory modalities.

The limbic system plays another important role in relation to sound.

Savan has proposed that sound stimulation of the limbic system is 'age specific'. As the limbic system of the brain is not fully developed until around two years of age, stimulation up to this point supports the development of coordination. If a child has not received adequate stimulation of the limbic system during this crucial time coordination remains undeveloped. In her studies, 80% of special-needs children had not received high frequency auditory stimulation during the first two years of life for a variety of reasons. Music is therefore perceived to be a 'whole brain' activity that stimulates the same areas used in reading processes. As Hodges states:

"Musical experiences are multimodal, involving auditory, visual, cognitive, affective, and motor systems." (Hodges 1996, p260)

Rhythm and Pre-verbal Development
Dyslexic children also appear to have problems:

"– remembering a melodic or rhythmic phrase and singing or clapping it back." (Miles and Miles, 1990, p49)

A key factor highlighted by Douglas and Willetts (1994) is the association between rhythmic ability and reading. They found that training in musical skills was a valuable strategy for assisting children with reading difficulties. This 'beat' detection, has been compared between dyslexic and non-dyslexic early readers by Goswami, who found that the dyslexic children were significantly less sensitive than the early readers to the 'stress beats' in speech. She writes:

"Children may benefit from focusing on the rhythmic patterns in language prior to learning to read." (Goswami, 2003, p465)

Knowledge of nursery rhymes is also strongly related to phonological skills (MacLean et.al 1987). In exploring the possible link between musical skills and reading, Douglas and Willetts (1994) found the combined aural measures (pitch and rhythm) correlated significantly with reading but not spelling. When they separated out the variable for vocabulary, they found that it was rhythm, rather than pitch, which significantly correlated with both reading and, to a lesser degree, spelling. Rhythm appears to be analysed in the left hemisphere of the brain, according to Borchgrevink (1982) while pitch, tonality, form and spatial perception are processed in the right hemisphere (Oglethorpe, 1996).

The Musical Brain and Infancy

Even within the womb musical (i.e. pitched) tones are recognised and familiarised by the unborn child. Trehub and others have shown that within weeks of birth very young infants can process and discriminate complex musical tasks, (Robertson, 1998, p19). Mallock, believes music is:

> " – hard-wired in all of us. It is not music in a cultural sense, but rather the energy that becomes music through our culture." (Mallock, 2003)

Working with Trevarthen, his observational studies of infant/mother communication utilise spectographic displays of sounds. He describes these as:

> "– 'extraordinarily regular' and 'equivalent to common time, 4:4' (or folk music) rhythmically, in a 'co-created relationship' between the mother/child dyad. (Mallock, 2003)

Trevarthan describes this pre-speech as 'highly musical in character' acting as a link between people which does not require language. It enables a uniting of people in group settings, across language barriers, and between mother and baby before language has developed. It is possible to have a fully co-ordinated, rhythmic 'conversation' with a baby without language, through human sensitivity for this pre-speech, rhythmic, relationship. The uniting role of music through pre-verbal (and non-verbal) communication is, according to Trevarthan:

> "At the very core of human vitality – it is what makes us human." (Trevarthan, 2003)

Practice

According to Oglethorpe the outstanding exponents of the multisensory approach to the teaching of music have been Emile Jaques-Dalcroze (1865-1950) and Zoltan Kodaly (1882-1967). These influences can be seen in the early-years educational practice of many European countries where formal literacy is not undertaken until the age of six-seven years. Instead, games, musical movements and expressions, together with vocal and listening skills are considered vital pre-cursers to formal literacy, to avoid cognitive damage and to ensure literacy flows in a developmentally appropriate way. Sylvia Hopland, head teacher of the Norwegian School in London, says:

> "We know that we could teach children to read at four if we wanted to but we want them to spend those years playing. Here (UK) you teach them to give the right answers. We want to teach them to solve problems, cooperate with others and cope with life." (Karpf, 2001)

Eurythmy

Oglethorpe credits Jaques-Dalcroze with the development of eurythmy through his efforts to broaden the basis of musical education. It was

Rudolph Steiner, however, who made eurythmy famous by giving it an integral part in his Waldorf wholistic educational practice. This system of coordinating music with bodily movement is practised throughout the Western world and Australia. Its primary object is:

> "– to create by the help of rhythm a rapid and regular current of communication between brain and body, and to make feeling for rhythm a physical experience" (Jaques-Dalcroze, 1930).

Of literacy Steiner wrote:

> "In reading, only the head and the intellect are engaged, and in a truly organic system of education we must develop everything out of the qualities and forces of the child's whole nature." (1981, p133)

Zoltan Kodaly

Although Kodaly, a Hungarian composer responsible for the re-establishment of music there in the 1950's, was motivated by a wish to re-introduce singing and music into education mainly for cultural reasons:

> "An unexpected result of the daily music instruction via the Kodaly method was a marked improvement of achievement in other academic areas." (Choksy, 1974, p.10)

Kodaly utilised existing Hungarian folk music and considered it equal in importance to academic subjects, language, mathematics and the social sciences. Kodaly found the pentaton – the five-tone scale – the ideal vehicle for teaching children musical skills and this is in fact also the basis of folk music in Hungary and most of the world.

Kodaly considered music to be a language which both pre-dated spoken or written language and which could convey things not possible in either of these. He believed it depended upon inner audition, and training the internal hearing, a view shared by standard musical instruction of a multisensory nature (Oglethorpe, 1996). Kodaly utilised singing, a shorthand notation of written music (Solfa scale) and hand-gestures in a developmentally appropriate, structured programme. This, he believed, reflected the patterns that follow normal child abilities at various stages of growth. As Choksy explains:

> "In terms of rhythm; moving rhythms are more child related than sustained ones. The quarter note is the child's walking pace, the eighth note, his running. These are the rhythms of the child's day-to-day living. His running games are largely made up of quarter- and eighth-note patterns in duple metre. They are a more reasonable starting place for teaching rhythm concepts to children than whole notes. Methodically, the first tones sung by young children are the minor third. They are the tones his mother uses to call him to dinner." (1974, p10)

There are other characteristics of the musical development of young children which play a part in the developmental sequence. These include accepting that the range and tones that young children can accurately sing are limited, and they should not be expected to sing in tune sounds which are developmentally beyond them.

Practice
Oglethorpe (1996) provides detailed instructions to teachers for using the piano with dyslexic children. Some general aspects of her practice follow:

Rhythm

The teacher and the pupil sit opposite each other with plenty of freedom to move both arms and legs from a sitting position. The teacher may begin by clapping or stamping or some similar, very simple, exercise. After a while the exercise is changed without breaking the continuity of movement. The initial movements should always be big and bold. Gradually all the limbs are involved. Then roles are changed with the teacher copying the child. If the child has left ear dominance, the first strategy in rhythm exercises (their weaker skill) is to have him listen with his right ear by asking him to close the left ear with the index finger of his left hand. If the pupil has right ear dominance, it is possible that rhythm per se will not be difficult but he may have difficulty with organising response to pitch and/or fitting rhythm and pitch together. These are worked at separately and broken down into very simple components.

Listening Skills

Pupils are encouraged to close their eyes and listen during silence for 2 minutes, although a dyslexic child may find 30 seconds, or one minute difficult. The child is asked to remember what sounds he has heard so that he can name them later. He is encouraged to count them on his fingers so that later on he can remember how many he is to remember.

Concept of 'Up' and 'Down'

The child sings slowly up the scale while accompanied on the piano, moving his hand slowly up from the abdomen and arriving at the top of his head and the top of the scale at the same time. He can then sing 'Up High' at the top of the octave and 'Down Low' at the bottom. A child may need to sing it, feeling each sound in his head and mouth, and to make the shape of it in the air as he sings.

Singing

Singing along to the music is encouraged. This helps to feel the shape of tunes and understand phrasing, giving a greater sense of progression. It is also good practice for memory and the breath control necessary for singing. It helps confidence, develops an awareness of pitch, and enables dyslexics to 'hear themselves'.

Klavar Musical Notation System

It is sometimes helpful for dyslexic children to utilise the Klavar system of written music. The dyslexic child will also be usually very good at pitch and can write their own melodies quite easily. These can be printed out on a computer programme, of which there are several, in Klavar style. The Klavar gives a more user-friendly image and shows the place on the keyboard while the traditional notation gives a symbol that needs to be interpreted before they can be found on the keyboard. Klavar therefore makes fewer demands on the memory. Klavar music notation system as available at: sales@klavarmusic.org. Information on Kodaly is at: www.britishkodalyacademy.org

The Steiner/Waldorf Schools website is: www.compulink.co.uk/-waldorf. Douglas and Willatts (1994) have researched the use of music-making with dyslexic children.

CHAPTER 6

PHARMOCOLOGICAL PROGRAMMES

There were 2 programmes in this category: pharmaceutical drugs and *Efalex* omega 3 essential fatty acids (EFAs) nutritional supplementation programme.

I   Pharmaceutical Drugs

Theory
There are four major classes of psychotropic medication: stimulants, tranquillisers, anticonvulsants and antidepressants. These include many drugs commonly prescribed for children with behavioural and/or learning disorders. Two types of drugs have been found to be particularly effective in dyslexia: the Nootropic drug *Piracetam* (Wilsher, 1996) and the Antihistamines (Levinson, 1980/1988). These have differing theoretical rationales but both aim to adjust the cognitive/mental behaviour of children at brain-chemical level.

A   *Piracetam*
Nootropic drugs are purported to improve memory and learning. *Piracetam* (20X0-1 pyrrolidine acetamide) was the first drug of this kind to be developed. It is a cyclic derivative of gamma-acetamide acid (GABA) an amino acid, but the exact action of the drug is unknown.

Piracetam was first used about 25 years ago in the treatment of memory problems in the elderly. It has been claimed that it selectively improves the efficiency of cognitive functions by increasing the turnover of ATP (adenosine triphosphate) which would increase the energy of cells. The use of the drug with children with learning disorders has a more recent history. It is thought that the drug improves the functioning of the left hemisphere of the brain and has few adverse effects (Wilsher, 1996, p141). Pinel, explains that of the four known amino acid neurotransmitters utilised in the brain, while the first three are common in the proteins we consume, GABA needs to be synthesised:

> "This is done by a simple modification of the structure of glutamate, which is the most prevalent excitatory neurotransmitter in the cerebral nervous system of mammals. GABA is the most prevalent inhibitory neurotransmitter in the brain". (Pinel, 1990, p97)

Pert (1997) whose work on neurotransmitters won her a Nobel Prize, explains that GABA is similar to serotonin, histamine, dopamine and other ligands in its action of enabling the brain to carry information across the synaptic gap between neurons.

She says:

> "Alcohol, tobacco, marijuana, cocaine and other drugs – all have natural analogs circulating in our blood, each of which binds to its very own receptor bodywide. Alcohol, for example, binds to the GABA receptor complex, which also accommodates Valium and Librium, common prescription drugs for quelling anxiety, providing an anti-anxiety effect, but only in the short run.

It is possible then, that *Piracetam* does the same thing and actually acts in an anti-anxiety capacity." (p299)

B   Antihistamines
In the late 1970's Harold Levinson MD suggested some dyslexics suffer from a cerebellar-vestibular (balance) disorder, which makes them prone to feelings of motion sickness. His theory is based on examination of many dyslexic children whom he concluded all had an inner ear disorder. This creates a problem with sensory communications between the inner ear to the cerebellar-vestibular mechanisms of the brain. They consequently experience problems with processing textual problems because the text appears to move. He advocated the use of antihistamine motion-sickness drug treatments including (trade names in brackets): cyclizine (*Marezine*), meclizine (*Antivert*), dimehydrinate (*Dramimine*), diphenydramine (*Benadryl*) and methylphenidate (*Ritalin*). Although the effect of antihistamines is said here to be solely as an anti-emetic to prevent nausea and motion sickness, histamine is a brain neurotransmitter so they may have a greater effect than this explanation suggests.

Levinson's theory of cerebellar involvement is supported by Stein, whose magnocellular theory is outlined in Chapter 3. He states:

> "Recently we, and others, have confirmed Dr Levinson's idea. – When we looked at the metabolism of cells in the cerebellum, we found a difference compared to normal readers." (In: Dobson, 2000)

These observations are also supportive of and linked to Nicolson and Fawcett's (1999) theory of the underlying role of the cerebellum in dyslexic children (discussed in Chapter 1). These researchers, known for their work on automaticity and its role in becoming literate, have argued that reading and spelling deficits are the surface consequence of a relative inability to automise skills. Consequently Pumfrey and Reason (1991) suggest that:

"– the possibility exists that drug treatment might improve the development of automaticity in children with specific learning difficulties (dyslexia)". (p178)

Practice

A   Piracetam is given by oral consumption, according to prescription, by a medical practitioner.

B   Levinson is an MD and so prescribes for his own clients. He also advises whichever herbal or nutritional supplements he considers indicated for each child.

One case study describes treatment as half of one antimotion-sickness drug per day plus ginkgo biloba and lecithin supplements. The treatment for this boy was expected to last 4-5 years.

Wilsher's 1996 paper provides further information on trials of Piracetam. Pumfrey and Reason (1991) also provide some information on the effectiveness of medical drugs.

Dobson (2000) gives further information on Levinson's cases, while Levinson (1991) has several case studies. More details of Levinson's Method are found at: www.dyslexiaonline.com/uk/treatment

II *Efalex*: Essential Fatty Acid Supplementation

Theory

Stordy and Nicholl's programme is based on the belief that children with dyslexia suffer a deficiency of the long chain polyunsaturated fatty acids (LCPs) required for normal, effective, rapid-fire communication between brain connections. LCPs are converted from the shorter chain essential fatty acids (EFAs). The authors state:

> "– you will suffer from an LCP deficiency unless your diet is rich in the foods containing the preformed LCPs." (Stordy & Nicholl, 2002, p17)

One such source is human breast-milk while another is fish oil which, in this model, forms the basis of the *Efalex* nutritional supplement programme.

The *Efalex* programme is based upon the research of Dr David Horrobin, an expert in EFAs, and Crispin Bennett. They found that four chromosomes and their gene sites bear anomalies in fatty acid membrane metabolism in children with dyslexia:

> "Genes send coded messages to cells instructing them to make specific proteins – such as muscle or – (the) enzymes that regulate the chemical reactions needed for growth, energy release and repair of tissues. – The positions on chromosomes that are linked with particular enzymes are identified by certain letters and numbers. These are a bit like identifying where a house is located on a street." (Stordy & Nicholl, 2002, p15)

The enzymes linked by Horrobin and Bennett (1999) with their associated chromosome sites are of two types, as shown in Table 3:

Table 3. Chromosome and enzyme links in dyslexia.

Chromosome	Gene Location	Enzyme
1	p36-34	Phospholipase A2
2	p15-16	
6	p23-21.3	Fatty Acid - CoA transferase
15	q21	Fatty Acid - CoA ligase

Transferase and ligase enzymes (on chromosomes 6 and 15) are associated with the incorporation of fatty acids into cell membranes. Phospholipases are associated with the breakdown of phospholipid membranes. (Phospholipids are the building blocks of brain cell membranes.) Both these processes must be in balance.

Stordy and Nicholl also quote the work of Galaburda and Livingstone (1993) and Stein and Walsh (1997) in suggesting areas of the brain affected in dyslexia:

"– it now appears that there are anomalies in the structure and function of those parts of the brain connecting the right and left hemispheres (the corpus callosum) and in the area of the brain involved in coordination and balance (the cerebellum). Dyslexic individuals also exhibit a level of disorganisation and reduced sensitivity in the magnocellular pathway within the brain, the large-cell superhighway responsible for the accurate high-speed perception of rapidly changing stimuli such as movement and sound variation." (Stein & Walsh 2002, p53)

However they do not accept these anomalies are genetically determined. Rather, they believe:

> "It is not just the genes that control how our body chemistry works, sometimes environmental factors interact with our genetic pre-disposition. Nutrition is one such environmental factor, and it has a strong bearing on how our genes influence our bodies." (2002, p17)

The Role of Fat

The authors maintain that the role of fat has been severely misunderstood in health as it has a crucial part to play. This applies in the functioning of the brain in particular, which is composed of 60% fat. However, the diet must contain sufficient of the right sort of fat: that which gives shorter-chain EFAs and, to a lesser extent, their longer-chain polyunsaturated fatty acid (LCP) derivatives. These are considered critical in brain health and, in particular, learning disorders.

There are two essential fatty acids: linoleic acid (LA) and alpha-linoleic acid (ALA) which are vitally involved in the proper functioning of every cell, tissue and organ in the human body. Like most vitamins these cannot be produced by the body so must come from the food we eat. LA is found in seed oils such as sunflower, safflower, corn and sesame. ALA is found in dark leafy vegetables, flaxseed oil and rapeseed oil. The human body cannot make LA from ALA, or vice versa, so must derive both from food. These two essential fatty acids have 18-carbon atoms in their molecule chains and must be converted into 22-carbon atoms in order to be fully utilised in the body. These molecules also have unsaturated bonds, sometimes called double bonds, between some of the carbon atoms. LA has two unsaturated bonds; ALA has three unsaturated bonds. The position of the first bond is biologically important and is named 'omega' or 'n'.

There are two main families of fats with more than one double bond. They are the omega-3 (or n-3) and omega 6 (or n-6) families, depending upon the position of the first double bond which is either 3-or 6-carbon atoms from the end of the chain. Through a series of transformations in the body ALA and LA are made longer or have more unsaturated bonds added. In the omega 6 family, LA (with 2 double bonds) is converted to arachidonic acid (AA) and adrenic acid (AdrA) which both have four double bonds and eventually becomes omega-6 docosapentaenoic acid (DPA) with five double bonds. In the omega-3 family ALA starts with three double bonds and is converted through several steps into eicosapentaenoic acid (EPA) with five double bonds and then docosahexaenoic acid (DHA) with six. Half of the fat in the brain is comprised of LCPs of which DHA is the most abundant omega-3 LCP. AA and AdrA are the most abundant omega-6 LCPs.

The process of conversion from one fatty acid to another, although controlled by enzymes can be slowed by many lifestyle factors including:

> "– typical Western diets rich in trans-fatty acids, stress, viral infections, too much alcohol and various illnesses." (Stordy & Nicholl, 2002, p82-3)

There are three main reasons for a lack of essential LCPs. The first is the deterioration of LCPs in the typical Western diet, in particularly changes in the last 100 years or less. For 4 million years human ancestors, as hunter-gathers, either ate a high proportion of oily fish or lived on fruit, nuts, herbs and animals. Stordy and Nicholl quote nutritional research by Broadhurst, Cunnane and Crawford (1998) which argues that this is the reason why humankind's superior brainpower did in fact evolve.

The African Rift Valley, where man is believed to have originated, is an area rich in enormous freshwater lakes providing an abundance of fish, crustaceans, molluscs and algae rich in the long-chain polyunsaturated fatty acids EPA, DHA and AA considered essential for efficient brain function. It is suggested almost 100% of our genetic structure evolved during this period. Today's common diet is therefore considered to be completely out of keeping with our genetic imprint. The ratio of omega-6 to omega-3 of the hunter-gathers would have been between 1:1 and 1:5. However, in modern times, the ratio is 10 to 12 times more omega-6 fatty acids than omega-3.

The hydrogenation of food, introduced about 12 years ago, in which trans-fatty acids are created in the process of hardening liquid vegetable oils into solid margarine or cooking fats, is given as the second main reason for this change. Trans fatty acids block the production of DHA, the omega-3 fat found in oily fish, and its precursor ALA. If the necessary omega-3 LCPs are not available, the body:

> "– has no choice but to make the most similar fat it can – the omega-6 DPA – from the fat that you've force-fed it. But the omega-6 DPA molecules are shaped differently from DHA. Your brain reluctantly takes the wrong fat and the result is akin to building a wall with bricks that don't fit, or trying to bake a cake without a major ingredient. The chemistry of the membrane around and within the nerve cells changes. The messages between the cells get scrambled and interrupted. Nothing works efficiently." (Stordy & Nicholl, 2000, p90)

The third major loss of omega-3 for the developing brain is due to the overall decline in breast-feeding leading to a serious deficiency in many people. A fully breast-fed infant receives all the protein, vitamins, minerals, carbohydrates and essential fatty acids and LCPs necessary. Breast-milk contains Arachidonic Acid (AA): the long-chain Omega 6 fatty acid necessary to achieve normal birth weight and head circumference as well as cardio-vascular development; Adrenic Acid (AdrA) the long-chain Omega 6 fatty acid made from AA in the body, and Docosahexaenoic Acid (DHA) the long-chain Omega-3 fatty acid, critical for the healthy development of the brain, central nervous system and vision.

The American Academy of Paediatrics and the American Dietetic Association recommendations are that a baby should be breast-fed for at least a minimum of one year although in America only 15% actually are while the UK has the lowest rate of breast-feeding in Europe, with almost one third of mother's not even trying (NCT, 2005). Many women now return to paid employment very soon after giving birth and this often necessitates an end to breast-feeding. This occurs in spite of the fact that breast-fed babies consistency show higher intelligence.

Breast-Fed Babies and Increased Intelligence
The authors cite several studies which support the view that breast-fed babies have statistically higher intelligence quotients (IQs) and improved visual perception compared with formula-fed infants. A major meta-analysis of twenty studies showed breast-fed babies scored 3-5 IQ points higher than their formula-fed counterparts. This took account of all possible variables including socio-economic status and education of the mother. It concluded breast milk was solely responsible for the cognitive advantages.

A study of three hundred children, all born prematurely, showed those given breast milk gained an 8-point higher IQ than those given formula. The children were aged 8 years when tested (Lucas, Morgan & Cole, 1992). Horwood and Fergusson (1998) found that breast-fed babies in the US were 38% more likely to grow up to successfully graduate from high school than their formula-fed counterparts. The LCP known as

DHA was found to be higher in the brains of breast-fed babies than those fed formula, showing dietary and brain levels of DHA are correlated. Studies with formulas, with or without added LCPs, have shown advantages for babies fed with those containing LCPs. Because of the low incidence of breast-feeding there is a call to include EFAs in baby-formula. The authors cite research from the *Pregnant physicians for DHA* group at Rockefeller University, New York, which concluded that:

> "– optimal brain development requires the DHA and AA provided by breast milk." (Stordy & Nichols, 2002, p99)

In addition to those in breast-milk, the unborn baby takes what essential fatty acids it needs from its mother while it is growing in utero. Therefore the mother's diet is also crucial during this time as well as after birth. However, Stordy and Nicholl express concern that even when babies are fed by their mothers, the mother's own diets are so lacking in the necessary omega-3 LCPs that the child does not receive an adequate supply. They conclude:

> "If we continue to eat the way we've been eating, there's little doubt that more and more children will suffer learning disorders of one kind or another." (2002, p102)

Meanwhile, their solution is the nutritional supplementation of EFAs.

Practice

Because it is not possible to eat sufficient of the food sources of LCPs to compensate for the severe depletion dyslexics experience, supplementation is considered necessary. *Efalex* was the commercial combination used in Stordy's trials (and those by Richardson and the Oxford University studies cited at the end of this chapter). *Efalex* is a largely fish-oil supplement rich in DHA. It uses tuna-fish oil, evening primrose oil, vitamin E and white thyme oil with a glycerine and gelatine capsule. Each capsule contains 60mg DHA (docosahexaenoic acid) 12 mg GLA (gamma-linolenic acid), 5.25 mg AA, (arachidonic acid) 1 mg thyme oil and 10 mg/15 IU natural source vitamin E.

Dose

The manufacturer's instructions are that adults and children aged 5 years and over require 4 capsules with food and drink daily. Children aged 2-5 years require 2- 4 four capsules with food and drink. Stordy and Nicholl recommend that if taking *Efalex* for the first time the above amounts should be doubled for the first 12 weeks, as substantial amounts are required to foster appreciable changes in dyslexic, dyspraxic or ADHD children. In earlier studies 480 mg of DHA a day was used which is also recommended by Stordy and Nicholl. This is 8 capsules per day for children over 5 and adults. Ideally, half the dose should be taken in the morning and half in the evening. If the child will not take the capsule or dislikes the taste the contents may be emptied into food or drink. The product is not suitable for children under 2 years. It is advised to consult a doctor if taking epilepsy drugs or if there is a history of epilepsy.

Length of Treatment

Initially this is for 12 weeks/3 months. After this time most users move onto a maintenance level of half the starting dose. While some individuals do see benefits before this time many have found it takes 12 weeks or longer, depending upon the individual. Factors such as growth spurts, which burn up the fatty acids as energy rather than allowing them to proceed to the membranes may cause this. Stordy and Nicholl stress that it is necessary to allow the full 3-month period in order to realistically evaluate the supplement programme.

Maintenance

Having moved to the maintenance level some people may notice some deterioration of their progress and then it is recommended to stick to the 480mg DHA dose per day. This may be necessary until after puberty as children may than require less.

Further support for the role of polyunsaturated fatty acids in dyslexics is given by Stein (2001), Taylor et.al (2000), Macdonnell et al (2000) and Stein and Walsh (1997). Researchers at Oxford University, UK, have both influenced and supported Stordy's hypothesis, in particular that of Richardson and her team (Richardson, McDaid, Calvin, et.al, (2000). At present no research is available to show how long the supplement is required.

CHAPTER 7

PHONOLOGICAL LITERACY PROGRAMME

One programme was included of this type: *Phono-Graphix*. This is a developmentally logical programme which differs significantly from the standard 'phonics' approaches currently emphasised in school settings.

Phono-Graphix

Theory
Phono-Graphix was developed by Carmen and Geoffrey McGuinness in the late 1990s. It asserts that dyslexia is the result of the wrong teaching policy and can be remedied by changing this. The authors describe reading as a code, which:

> "– maps 26 symbols to nearly 40 sounds. – It was obvious to us – that the missing piece of reading instruction was code knowledge. -When you let go of the notion that you must match sounds to letters, and begin to see the letter patterns as pictures of sounds, the code was perfectly predictable and all the instructional issues began to melt away." (McGuinness & McGuinness, 1998, pix-x)

The usual reason given for persistent de-coding problems is that there is something wrong with the individual's brain (the phonological core deficit theory). In *Phono-Graphix* this premise is rejected. The authors believe the term 'learning disabilities' is often a euphemism for 'can't read' and that detailed reports and statistics analysed in the USA and UK literacy tables show that a child's and, ultimately, an adult's reading problem, are caused by the educational system and not because there is something wrong with poor readers:

> "It is impossible that 30-60% of school children have an inherent, i.e. brain-based deficit leading to reading failure, and in any case, reading and spelling are not biological properties of our human brain." (McGuinness, 1998, p12)

Of current phonics instruction McGuinness states:

> "The orientation from letter to sound is wrong – the sounds in our language existed long before the letters. The written symbols of our language were invented to represent the sounds we had been making for centuries. Phonics instruction is driven from the letter to the sound, as if the sounds exist to suit the letters. This direction of instruction fails to allow the child to use what he already possesses, the sounds. He is completely intimate with his language – for him to learn to read, he needs instructional activities which encourage him to learn the symbols that were invented to represent the sounds that – he already knows. This knowledge is like a magical key to written language. – Phonics throws away the key and starts from scratch teaching him the sounds as if they were something new." (McGuinness, 1998, p11)

She concludes:

"People are illiterate because none of the current methods of
reading instruction work for everyone." (p12)

After an exhaustive review of the research on dyslexia the authors of
Phono-Graphix reject the idea of dyslexia as a learning disability,
having taken remedial children who have been thus diagnosed and
taught them to read in 12 hours. In a revue of other remedial systems
they found only one was successful (the Lindamood ADD programme)
and this also used the logic of the code and was able to teach everyone to
read. Consequently, they state:

"There is only one right way to teach an alphabetic writing
system." (McGuinness, 1998, p220)

And that, based on their research, any child who is not mentally retarded
or deaf can be taught to read if given the proper instruction.

Developmental Logic
Phono-Graphix rests on the assumption that reading must be taught
according to the logic of the code. With the English language this
comprises the sound-pictures of the 26 letters and approximately 40
phonemes. As discussed, current reading methods based on either
phonetics or whole-words do not follow the logic of the English
alphabetic code and they also require children to perform logical
thinking for which they are developmentally immature. For example,
McGuinness and McGuinness describe how *paired associate learning*,
where a letter such as <t> represents a sound 't' or the letter <p>
represents the sound 'p', as used in phonetics, is very difficult for young
children because it is meaningless to them.

In addition, the use of rules to teach the sounds that groups of letters
represent relies on *prepositional logic* to explain 'if this, then that'

situations. For example, the long <ai> in the word 'rain' would be explained using the rule that when two vowels are side by side they represent the long sound of the first letter. However, this rule is not only difficult to follow but frequently wrong, when it is then considered an exception. In fact this rule only works in English 40% of the time. Exceptions are found in the words 'mountain,' 'captain' and others. McGuinness and McGuinness write:

> " – we have the rule working 40% of the time and the exception working 60% of the time. As if this isn't confusing enough, phonics also teaches adjacent consonants as units. So instead of leaving a child alone once he knows the sound to symbol relationship of sounds like 'f' and 'r', it goes on to teach him 'fr' as if it were something altogether different. So now he has three things to remember <f>, <r>, and <fr>."
> (1998, p7)

They describe how phonics is the result of non-developmentally contingent rules and regulations that by the late 1970s gave an illiteracy rate of around 33% in the USA and even more in the UK.

The early 1980s saw the introduction of the 'Whole Language' movement ('Real Books' in the USA). The theory behind this was that children do not need to know the code in order to read, (partly because it is too unpredictable) so the phonics method was rejected. They believed instead the child could recognise words as she did objects. Children were expected to 'emerge' into literacy from this. However, the authors refute this is possible:

> "Children do not recognise whole words like they recognise other familiar objects in their visual world. – In fact, reading isn't even based on a visual stimulus but on an oral one, the

sound. It is the sounds that our forefathers were attempting to represent when they invented the written code, not the other way around." (McGuinness & McGuinness, 1998, p8)

The result educationally was a mixture of phonics and whole-books which, when found to be ineffectual, resulted in the current call for the return of phonics.

But, according to the authors, the current version of phonics:

> "– teaches only about 50% of the alphabetic code, and teaches that 50% using methods that are logically inappropriate to a child under 9 years of age." (McGuinness & McGuinness, 1998, p10)

According to the authors of *Phono-Graphix*, developmental psychologists have known for 50 years that children under 9 years cannot manage prepositional logic or handle contingent thinking very well. They consequently become thoroughly confused attempting to learn something for which they are developmentally un-ready. McGuinness and McGuinness accept that there is something right about both phonics and whole-word teaching. The promotion of literature and reading in the child's environment is approved. And, while the importance of teaching phonetics is recognised, this is all it has right and from then on it is:

> "– confusing, often wrong and developmentally inappropriate to young children" (McGuinness & McGuinness, 1998, p11)

The Sub-Skills of Reading

There is great stress placed in *Phono-Graphix* on the *sub-skills of reading* (these are the skills necessary if reading is going to be successful). Indeed, this is all that the authors feel children of 4-5 years need to be taught initially. *Phono-Graphix* teaches the following sub-skills:

1   Ability to scan text from left to right. Children of 5 and older can understand that the code moves in one direction. They may need reminding from time to time.

2   Ability to match visual symbols to auditory sounds, such as the symbol <t> = the sound 't'. Children of 5 and older can do this paired associate learning as long as relevance is added to the formula. *Phono-Graphix* teaches only 8 sound pictures at a time, using those sound pictures to read and spell real words. By using these 8 sound pictures, children begin to understand why they need to know the code.

3   Ability to blend discrete sound units into words. They found children of 5 and older can blend sounds into words once they have been shown by example, what is expected of them.

4   Ability to segment sounds in words. Children of 5 and older can segment sounds in words once shown by example what is expected of them.

5   Ability to understand that sometimes two or more letters represent a sound; for example 'sh'. Children of 5 and older can understand that sometimes sound pictures are made with two letters. They cannot understand this by imposition of a prepositional rule but they easily understand that sometimes it just happens. In a Kindergarten study the authors proved this by using the same logic with 40, 6-year old children in

which all 40 answered 'a house' when combining the two separate elements of a triangle and a square:

6   Ability to understand that most sounds can be represented in more than one way. For example, the sound 'ee' can be spelled in several ways: green, team, happy etc. The authors have demonstrated that 6 year-olds easily understood that things can have the same name and not be exactly alike, so they can also know that <ee>, <ea> and <y> can all be pictures of the sound 'e'.

These 6 elements comprise a set of sub-skills that, once the reader becomes adept, become unconscious. McGuinness (1998) states that these sub-skills have been shown to be necessary for a child or adult to master any alphabetical writing system and that children's linguistic and logical development (their cognitive development) are of critical importance in setting up the proper sequence of instruction. That is, it is vital to follow the child's own development and that the child must be logically (cognitively) ready for reading.

1:1 Adult/Child Interaction

Two other factors which assist children in learning reading are also stressed in *Phono-Graphix*: talking to the child from babyhood, regardless of whether they appear to understand, and the 1:1 adult/child relationship. The authors found that even though *Phono-Graphix* is successful in whole-class situations and small groups it is even more so in 1:1 situations.

Practice

Following extensive research with remedial as well as new readers (children and adults) the authors developed a method which, they say, can teach a person to read in 12 hours and some in less time. Although anyone of any age can learn to read and spell using *Phono-Graphix*, McGuinness and McGuinness have written *Reading Reflex: the foolproof Phono-Graphix method to teach your child to read* specifically for parents. This is a user-friendly, spiral bound workbook which prepares a parent to teach *Phono-Graphix* and provides everything necessary to follow it in the correct order and style. Individual lesson plans are each divided into the same sections: a *readiness* section which advises suitability; a *goals* section describing exactly what the goals of the lesson are; *materials* and *presentation* sections – the latter being laid out in clear steps guiding parent and child through the lesson plan; *correcting problems* and *variations on presentation*.

The Pre-Test

This is the preliminary step of the course. It has four elements: a blending test; phoneme segmentation test; auditory processing test and a code knowledge test. Together these give a composite score. The authors stress stopping any test if the child cannot give 3 consecutive answers correctly as this will indicate the total score. They advise that the auditory processing test is not developmentally appropriate for a child less than half way through year one of school.

Literacy Growth Chart

A *Literacy Growth Chart* is provided to illustrate goals for the child, but it is stressed that these are goals to aim at rather than 'norms'.

Teaching The Basic Code.

McGuinness and McGuinness describe the *basic code* as:

> "– the most common sounds, and those sounds that are represented by only one letter. Teaching your child the reading mechanics needed to manage the basic code will establish the way she responds to all future text as well."

(1998, p53)

The goals of teaching the *basic code* are that the child understands that letters are picture sounds and that she knows the correspondence between all the sounds and sound pictures that make up the *basic code*. A distinction is made for children under 6 who:

> "– often lack the left to right orientation needed to distinguish between the sound pictures <d> and <b>."
> (McGuinness & McGuinness, 1998, p57)

Further goals are: that the child understands that spoken words are made up of sounds; that she understands that written words are made up of sound pictures which represent the sounds in words; that she understands that the sound pictures in written words occur in a sequence that she is able to segment into the sounds in spoken words; is able to sequence from left to right, and that she is able to blend the sounds in words.

The lessons plans are: 'The Blending Game'; 'Finding Sounds Around Us'; 'Three-Sound Word Building'; 'Three-Sound Auditory Processing'; 'Sound Bingo'; 'Three-Sound Directed Reading'; 'Three-Sound Spelling Practice' and 'Reading Stories in Basic Code'. Each contains resources to cut up and use with the lesson. At the end of the *basic code* section, advice is given for next steps for younger children and in continuing into teaching *Adjacent Consonant Sounds*. The same section structure for each lesson plan is retained.

'Word families' are not recommended as this prevents children learning to de-code their language, encouraging guessing and learning to rhyme, rather than learning the meaning of the sound-pictures. McGuinness and McGuinness argue that the English language is not intended to be spoken in sound units or consonant-vowel word families, as:

> "our written language was intended as a sound picture code,
> not a word family code to be memorised in little arbitrary
> chunks. So, instead of wasting precious visual memory on
> redundant information, we teach children to blend sounds
> together, not to remember them as a unit." (1998, p158)

They also consider it would be overloading the child's visual memory
to teach all the possible consonant-consonant combinations and, as no
new information is being introduced, it is only logical to 'chunk' them;
a word they use with the child to distinguish what they are doing from
syllables. As recalling all the sounds in longer words when blending is
a challenge to the child's short–term memory, they suggest re-doing
the *basic code* if the child is taking a very long time. The next lesson
plans are: 'Word Building With Adjacent Consonants'; 'Directed
Reading With Adjacent Consonants'; 'Spelling Practice with Adjacent
Consonants' and 'Reading Stories That Contain Adjacent Consonants'.

The Advanced Code
Again, the sub-skills necessary before embarking on the next stage of
reading are clearly shown and the goals of this stage given. These are:
the ability to understand that sometimes two or more letters represent a
sound; the ability to understand that most sounds can be represented in
more than one way, including a plan for organising new information: Of
this the authors state:

> "Giving the child new information is only one job of
> education. Giving him a plan for organising that information
> is just as important. Without that, he cannot possibly
> understand and retain the new information."(McGuinness &
> McGuinness, 1998, p208)

And thirdly, the ability to understand that there is overlap in the code, that some components of the code can represent more than one sound including a child-led strategy for managing the overlap, in a similar way as in goal 2. Lesson plans for these 3 goals are: Word Building With Advanced Code; Practising Common Consonant Sound Pictures; Mapping And Sorting; Vowel + e; Sound Sorting; Word Analysis; Scratch Sheet Spelling (a strategy); Reading Coded Texts and Sound Search.

Multi-Syllable Management

Following the *Advanced Code* the authors re-cap on the sub-skills the child will now have learnt and then state:

> "Many parents and reading methods stop here, never offering the child directed instruction or guided experience in the management of multi-syllable words. This is a big mistake." (1998, p295)

They stress that in the processing of reading children are building from the sounds to the syllables to the meaning (the word) so must use methods which teach them to build words from smaller sound parts to the whole word and that anything else is illogical.

Age-Appropriate Guidance

The authors provide a general rule-of-thumb for parental expectations:

> "– If your child is older than year one, six months (of school) make your way through the lessons until they start to get too difficult for her. A good rule of thumb is that year two pupils should be able to read and spell two-syllable words, year three pupils should be able to read and spell three-syllable words, and children older than that should be

able to read and spell four-syllable words whose meanings
they know." (McGuinness & McGuinness, p308)

To distinguish work for younger children or new readers, (those of year
1 + 6 months or younger) a flying *Sound Doggy* symbol appears on
suitable lesson plans. The course concludes with some general
recommendations to parents, including reading aloud for about 30
minutes a day with a child under 10 years of age, or until the child has
been reading fluently for about a year; what to read and, finally, a retest
using tests provided in the book.

Complete details on *Phono-Graphix* and how to teach using it are in
McGuinness and McGuinness (1998). Additional information and
research support for *Phono-Graphix* can be found at *Read America*
www.readamerica.net/research

CHAPTER 8

HOW THE STUDY WAS CARRIED OUT

As I described in Chapter 1, the field of dyslexia is conflicted and confused. There are three major theories of the possible cause and yet only one of these – the phonological core deficit theory – is related to current practice. In addition, some practice is based purely on what has been found historically to be useful – the multisensory approach – but lacks an adequate explanation for why this works. There are also many successful and diverse programmes for helping children with dyslexia, including those of a non-literary nature, which are not incorporated into current practice. And this is despite the fact that some are supported by a major theory – the cerebellar theory – of dyslexia. But how can such diverse programmes all be successful and would understanding this help clear the confusion?

Grounded Theory

To pursue these questions it was decided to start by studying what actually helps children with dyslexia. By adopting this 'bottom-up' approach, rooted in children's experiences of what had helped them and practitioners' understanding of their programmes, we might be able to learn something new about dyslexia itself. The methodology adopted to achieve this was *grounded theory*. This is designed to enable new meaning to be made from real-life experience and, from this, new theoretical ideas to be developed. Any new insights or hypothesis generated would therefore be 'grounded' in what has been shown to work in practice.

The research asked:

> Do successful programmes of dyslexia share common elements of theory and practice and, if so, what can we learn about dyslexia from these?"

The study's design was an adaption of work by Lauren Resnick (1987) in which a variety of educational programmes were analysed for their effectiveness:

> "I looked for elements common to successful programmes that could point cumulatively towards a theory of how learning and thinking skills are acquired." (p18)

A similar over-view across the 14 successful programmes for dyslexia outlined in Chapters 2-7 took place and a hypothesis generated from what was found to be the shared elements across them. The study was not intended as a measure of which programme was superior or more effective, but as a search for common elements across diverse, successful programmes. Because many countries do not use the term *Dyslexia* and those which do vary in how they assess children and/or apply the term they use for reading problems, it was decided to include programmes where practitioners' research samples had been assessed using either the 'discrepancy' criterion – where the child's reading ability appears to lag 2 years or more behind what one might expect from their general intelligence – or where users were described as 'dyslexic' by practitioners, children or their parents. Terms such as 'reading disability' (used in the JST programme for example) were found to be equivalent to 'dyslexia'.

Participants

As described in Chapter 1, the aim of the study was to include as diverse a range of programmes as possible. This meant many programmes similar to the 14 described were excluded. Some of these other programmes were, however, explored in the light of the study findings (see Chapter 10).

Procedure

Grounded theory's aim to 'make meaning' requires repeated returning to the original data in the light of what is being generated by the assessment. The steps for this process are shown in Fig. 9.

Step 1

Multi-rich data was gathered on each programme. This was drawn from a variety of sources: semi-structured interviews, instructional videos, web pages, books, journal and magazine articles, promotional information and personal correspondence together with research support for each programme. This included published personal advocacy (case-study) as well as quantitative analyses.

Step 2

The collective data formed a *Model* of each programme. In each of these the Theory and Practice of the programme was described. Chapters 2-7 of this book represent 'potted' descriptions of these (complete *Model* data is available in Poole 2005). Information on theory and practice was presented in practitioner's own spoken or written words and without

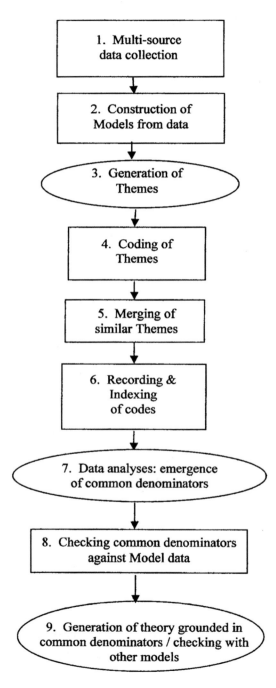

Fig 9. The Grounded Theory Procedure in this Study

critique. This was to prevent accidentally changing the meaning of what was being said or done within the programme and thus losing the 'active ingredients'. Where a semi-structured interview had taken place the *Model* was returned to the practitioner for validation before analysis to ensure it was an accurate account.

Steps 3 & 4

In order to find a way of looking for shared ingredients in the theory and practice of programmes, it was necessary to represent the raw data in the *Models* in a way which could be analysed. To do this, *Themes* in the text were underlined and given a shorthand code. An example of coded text can be seen in Figure 10 below. Themes were either names of brain parts, the sense being focused upon, or concepts which sought to encapsulate what practitioners were describing.

This sample of text from Stein's coloured overlay programme shows: V (theme-code for the visual sense); S (theme-code for the Sensory concept); Cb (theme-code for the Cerebellum); MGC (theme-code for the Magnocellular system); IH (theme-code for the inner hearing/speech concept); Vc (theme-code for the vocal sense); and BR (theme-code for

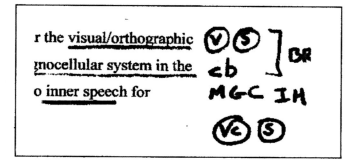

Fig 10. An Example of Coded Text

brain region/activity, used to identify text sequences describing brain information). Each theme-code was listed on a *memo sheet* for the programme as it was generated and the same theme codes used for further programmes until all the *Model* text had been coded. Frequency of themes was not recorded as this was unimportant, but only their presence in the programme. Where a sense (auditory, visual, touch, oral, vestibular) was highlighted in the data, it was given its own theme-code and also that for the generic *Sensory* (S) to note the presence of sensory as a concept. Where several senses appeared in the text together, they were also double-coded for the *Multisensory* (MS) Theme.

Step 5

Where themes had been coded for very similar concepts, (for example, *Learning Style/Dominance Profile* and *Balance/Orientation)* they were merged so that scoring would not be divided between them, inadvertently diluting the presence of the theme. (All merged codes are given in Appendix I.) Finally, the entire coding procedure was repeated to ensure consistency and accuracy of theme-codes.

Step 6

Following this step 126 different *Themes* had been generated (these are listed in Appendix II). In addition the page and line number of each theme's location within the *Models* was indexed and filed to create an *audit trail* (Pidgeon, 1996, p84).

Step 7. Common Denominators

Themes were analysed using a *repertory grid*. This worked by listing themes vertically and programmes horizontally, entering a score of 1 for the presence of each theme against each programme on the grid. A score of 14 across an entire row (i.e. all programmes) indicated the theme was shared and was therefore a *common denominator* (CD). The CDs for Practice and Theory are shown below in Table 4:

Table 4. Common Denominators of Successful Programmes

Practice CDs

Theory CDs

Sensory (S)	(12)
Visual Sense (VS)	(11)
Non-Literary Dyslexia	(11)
Orientation (O)	(10)

Sensory (S)	(14)
Brain Region (BR)	(14)
Orientation (O)	(13)

Practice CDs

In the table above, the theme *Non-Literary Dyslexia* (NLD) is used to indicate a non-literary programme or definition of dyslexia. This was interesting as its presence as a CD suggests that, a) there is more to dyslexia than a purely literary problem and, b) literary programmes may therefore not be the only or best way to approach helping children with dyslexia. Because the NLD code was a label, representing a description rather than a concept, it was not used directly in the hypothesis-building stage. However, its presence lends great support to the resulting hypothesis of dyslexia (described in detail in Chapter 9). The code (V) represents the visual sense, which in a visual reading problem such as dyslexia is not in itself a very surprising theme and it too was therefore not utilised in the hypothesis generating stage of the study. This left the 2 concept themes *Sensory* (S) and *Orientation* (O) as the common denominators for the Practice section.

Theory CDs

In the Theory table the theme for *Brain-Region* (BR) again represented a description in the text whenever a brain area or brain activity was highlighted. In the original study this information was used to build a new understanding of brain activity in dyslexia and was not part of the hypothesis building process. This meant that the common denominators (CDs) for the Theory section were *Sensory* (S) and *Orientation* (O). The CDs were therefore the same for both Theory and Practice. (A full discussion of these results can be found in Poole 2005). Once again, referring back to the original data enabled more meaning to be made of the findings:

The *Sensory* CD
Sensory as a theme was coded when any individual sense was referred to in a programme. So, although the sensory focus varied among programmes, *Sensory* as a concept retained a shared emphasis. The presence of *Sensory* through 12 Model's Practice sections and all 14 Theories was therefore thought significant. *Sensory* was however, un-coded in the Practice sections of the two pharmacological programmes. Both of these comprised simple prescriptive instructions for taking either medication or Omega 3 EFAs and so could not realistically have been given a code for the *Sensory* concept. This highlights a possible shortcoming of the study's methodology in that those programmes where the practice is a simple 'prescription' may not carry their implicit themes through into the Practice data, but those that described their reasoning again in the Practice section, probably would, and so be coded and scored.

That *Sensory* should be present as a theme in every programme's theory section is not perhaps a surprising result. The brain is a sensory organ in which every area but the frontal lobes is dedicated to processing various forms of sensory information. (And even these may perform some sensory functions, Kolb & Whishaw, 1996). What did appear surprising however, was the high profile of the *Sensory* theme in the results, given its low profile in current major theories of dyslexia.

The *Orientation* CD

This theme is in 13 of the 14 Theory sections. Because the code for *Orientation* (O) was used to cover a number of similar meanings in the text it was important to ensure these had been legitimately grouped together. (Appendix III shows all examples of text coded for the *Orientation* theme.) On returning to the text once more, it was found that all but 2 programmes coded for this theme discuss either 'spatial awareness' and/or 'bodily awareness in gravity', or 'sensory confusion' and/or 'perceptual instability' in their theories. Of the other 2, *Phono-Graphix* and Irlen's SSS programme, it is said that children often, 'lack the orientation needed to distinguish between sound pictures <d> and <b>'. Theirs is therefore a purely literary disorientation, as opposed to the previous examples. So, while it could be argued that this use of the *Orientation* theme is applied somewhat differently from the other examples, it nevertheless raises the suggestion that 'disorientation' could be expressed at a purely cognitive/thinking level.

Of the 14 Practice sections the theme of *Orientation* is coded in 10, the four exceptions being Bakker's Balance Model, *Efalex*, JST and *Alpha to Omega*. In Bakker's Model the child simply sits with headphones while undertaking prescriptive literary tasks depending upon which hemisphere is being alluded (stimulated). Likewise *Alpha to Omega* is a series of literary exercises. The Practice section of JST describes the provision of a tape/CD of music for the child and *Efalex* a pill to swallow. Again, this suggests there is a limit to some themes being coded in the Practice, despite their presence in a programmes' Theory section.

Bakker was the only programme that had no coding for *Orientation* in either the Practice or Theory sections. A closer study of the data showed that only its title gave any reference to 'balance' or 'orientation' themes, but that this itself should perhaps have received the *Orientating* theme code. Bakker's theory is that the child develops first right-hemisphere and then both hemisphere (balanced) functioning as s/he learns literacy: a concept certainly in keeping with the very similar theme of *Orientation*. After re-examining the original data together with the 2 CDs, it was therefore felt, that the concept of *Orientation* as either implicit or explicit in the theory and practice of the 14 successful programmes appeared to be supported, and that it was valid to pursue these in the hypothesis-building phase of the study.

It was particularly significant that both the Practice and Theory sections of the programmes should have the same common denominators, lending even more congruence to the results.

Generation of a New Hypothesis

The second stage of the grounded theory process was the generation of a new hypothesis based upon the two shared elements (common denominators): *Sensory* and *Orientation*. Because this was grounded in successful theory and practice, any new hypothesis had the potential to offer new and possibly unifying insights to the field of dyslexia. Chapter 9 explores the hypothesis that was generated.

CHAPTER 9

ORIENTATION: WHAT IS IT?

Although balance has a prominent place in Nicolson and Fawcett's cerebellar theory of dyslexia, which was described in Chapter 1, the concept of *Orientation* is not something currently much discussed. Orientation is more than balance. Orientation is the result of adapting to life in a gravitational environment. It comes about through the triangulation of incoming multisensory information. Touch and pressure; sensation from the skin, muscle and tendons; visual and motor information from the brain, and data about balance from the inner ear and vestibular organs must all integrate to provide orientation. Sensory and motor impulses are both sent and received by the thalamus, to and from the cerebellum. But because the cerebellum acts only as a *moderator* between the vestibular (balance) system and the cortex, and the thalamus a relay station for sensory information, it appears unlikely that either the cerebellum or the thalamus are in themselves the 'cause' of the observed behaviours of dyslexia but are related elements within a wider network of disorientation. As Nicolson and Fawcett observe:

> "It would be premature to assign difficulties to the cerebellum alone owing to its rich interconnections with cerebral cortex and thalamic nuclei". (1999, p172)

Clearly, if the magnocellular pathways of the thalamus, or to and from the cerebellum, are undernourished, and/or do not process sensory information smoothly, problems within the whole sensory processing system will result. Indeed, if any element interferes with the processing, integration and formation of associations between sensory stimuli, disorientation is likely.

Sensory Integration and Dys-Synchronicity

In multisensory processing, information flows simultaneously through different brain areas over multiple neurological systems: known as 'parallel processing'. This repeated firing in unison is what establishes associations between stimuli and results in the neurological pathways that create new learning and automatic responses. As this occurs the limbic system registers and stores the emotional meaning/s to the associated stimuli for future reference so that a memory record is made for later speed of response. Therefore it is the functioning of the sensory system as a whole that enables multisensory processing of all incoming stimuli and thus orientation.

For successful reading to occur the brain areas must 'communicate' and operate as a whole system involving precise neural timing. In dyslexia it appears that the brain is unable to process incoming sensory stimuli as an integrated whole and the multisensory pathways necessary for automatic learning may consequently fail to 'fire' and be laid down. Evans and Park (1995) refer to this lack of multisensory firing as 'interrupting synchronicity'. When they measured quantitative EEG readings in dyslexic individuals they found 'decreased communication' between areas specific to reading, concluding:

> "– persons with specific reading disabilities – might be
> referred to more basically as 'dysynchronous persons' (p25).

Once 'disorientated' the mechanisms of sensory processing, which would otherwise enable orientation, maintain a self-perpetuating state of disorientation, as the dys-synchronous signals remain un-integrated. The cerebellum may now both receive and/or relay un-integrated information to and between other brain areas.

This situation will remain until something acts to interrupt the disorientation. For example, in Stein's programme outlined in Chapter 3 lack of bifocal convergence sends out conflicting visual sensory messages resulting in dyslexic symptoms. Occlusion of one eye removes the conflicting signals enabling one visual pathway to become dominant, preventing the disorientation. Alternatively, the underlying sensory integration problem may be addressed as in the DORE and PRI programmes in Chapter 4.

Interestingly, Ayres (1982/91) has always proposed that sensory integration problems are at the root of many developmental disorders and, prior to the 'phonological core deficit' theory described in Chapter 1, Birch (1962) advocated a sensory integration theory of dyslexia. Research aimed at demonstrating this was however compounded by its literary nature and it was also not possible to tell if it was the individual senses or the integration between them which was the problem. Consequently, the theory was abandoned (Vellutino, 1979). Recently, however, Hairston and his colleagues, using non-literary stimuli, have found a sensory integration problem to be central in dyslexia. Their participants required a longer time frame in which to associate visual and auditory sensory information, experiencing poor integration of multisensory information at a 'pre-linguistic' stage (Hairston et. al 2005, p15). This suggests Birch's original proposal was largely accurate.

Literacy and Orientation

In order to fully understand how a disorientated child may experience difficulty with literacy, it is important to appreciate that literacy is entirely culturally developed and not in any way 'natural'. Unlike speech, which does appear to be innate in humans – developing in interactive processes with the environment – there is no innate literary scheme in humans. Consequently, although frequently referred to as such (e.g. Blakemore & Frith, 2005, p76) and illustrated in Fig 11 below, there is no such thing as a 'reading brain' with a 'reading brain system'. There is, however an 'orientating brain' for which the sole function of processing sensory information is to maximise survival.

Orientation is knowing where one is in relation to the environment and what it contains in order to respond appropriately. Indeed, orientation *is* this relationship. This means that all sensory processing is a contextual, relational activity. That is, it is *ecological* – where the individual must assess the situation and decide in what position to place itself for best survival. For until the brain understands its relationship with the incoming stimuli (good or bad, run away, eat, hide or attack, etc) it cannot know how to respond. Sensory perception is the means of enabling this.

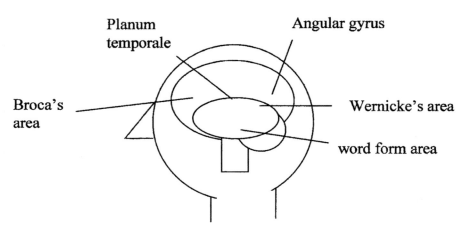

Fig. 11 The Brain's 'Reading System'.

Speech, for example, is usually perceived as coming from somewhere. Human auditory stimuli from two offset ears will be processed by the orientating areas of the brain while their meaning to the individual (via the limbic system) is perceived. The same is true for visual and tactile stimuli. Literacy is therefore a multisensory activity, dependent upon the efficiency of underlying sensory processing structures, which has been artificially mapped onto a 'survival brain'. So, while it is true that areas of the brain are 'adopted' during literacy, one cannot separate literacy acquisition from orientation.

Orientation and the Parietal Lobe

Interestingly, Blakemore and Frith (2005) cite Eden's research (see p93) which found young adults with dyslexia used the parietal (orientating) lobe of the cortex to help integrate visual and auditory stimuli. Evans and Park (1995) also found that 'abnormalities' occurred in the parietal (orientation) areas in 70% of their dyslexic sample. The parietal lobes – especially the right – are responsible for the integration of incoming sensory information including the 'body-map'. Blakemore and Frith suggest that this is a 'different area' from the one they are meant to use according to the reading areas usually designated to the brain. But as I have suggested, it is misleading to label specific areas as such. It may be that some children have brains which are more 'orientating'. These could be the 'holistic' thinkers Stein refers to in Chapter 3. Alternatively, some might require literary education that is more tactile and/or naturally more grounded in physical activity. It could also be that literacy with a confusing code might, in certain children, evoke their parietal lobe in an attempt to remain orientated rather than confused.

Disorientation may also be one of the possible causes of 'left neglect,' which Stein noticed in many children with dyslexia. Two explanations for this phenomenon have been suggested: one that it is caused by 'defective sensation or perception' and, two that it is caused by 'defective attention or orientation' (Kolb and Wishaw 1996, p275). The parietal regions are responsible for integrating spatial information connected with movement, orientation, calculation and certain types of recognition. Therefore, if there is an integrative area of the brain in terms of orientation of all sensory information, the parietal lobe – in particular the inferior parietal lobe of the right hemisphere – appears the most likely. This is further supported by recent research into *dyscalculi* a problem which affects the rapid processing of numerical information in about 5% of the population. This, like dyslexia, is therefore a sensory de-synchronisation problem but its cause has been considered a mystery. In this study it was found that the right parietal lobe is probably the seat of dyscalculia (Cohen Kadosh, 2007). This suggests a similar inability to map numeracy onto a disorientated brain might apply in these cases, with a similar solution.

Current research is combining to suggest that, if only for those with dyslexia, orientation is a key element in sensory integration during literacy. And, because one cannot separate literacy acquisition from orientation, factors which interfere with the efficient processing of an orientating brain are increasingly relevant in understanding how dyslexia could result. These may include poor nutrition, (low Omega 3 EFAs) or individual differences of brain 'wiring' (dominance profile or learning style). And although areas of the brain may become utilised for the processing of elements of literacy, it does not follow that those who use different areas are using the 'wrong' part. If dyslexic children have more 'orientating' brains due to their different brain style, they may simply possess a different *genetic identity.*

Genetic Identity

Accepting the concept of brain difference rather than brain fault allows an interpretation of dyslexia that does not pathologise the child. A 'different' processing pattern need not constitute a 'faulty' brain but rather a naturally different arrangement of pathways and sensory emphasis. This can be thought of as a child's *genetic identity* (GI). Different children might therefore require different environmental elements or sensory input in order to fully orientate. A variety of environmental factors might potentially interact with the individual GI of the child giving a *multi-factorial* explanation for dyslexia. This could also explain the fact that no single gene is consistently associated with literary problems and provide a re-interpretation of the role of those genes that have been linked.

Pathways to Dyslexia

There could therefore be many pathways to dyslexia where the individual needs of the particular child have simply not been recognised and/or met. For example, a child who was a visual thinker (possible a connection with chromosome C15) could become cognitively disorientated by the English Orthography itself, which is known to be confusing and illogical. S/he could instead be taught using a more visual system. Likewise a child with immune-system damage (a link to chromosome C6) might experience magnocellular problems which could result in whole body/mind disorientation. Any child who had received insufficient Omega 3 EFAs might also exhibit this type of disorientation.

Alternatively a child who had failed to internalise phonemes in speech prior to literacy, due to glue-ear or auditory inflammation when an infant (C6) could likewise experience cognitive confusion when learning literacy. A left-handed child (connected with chromosome C2) might also require a specific reading system to be able to fully orientate. And, because hemisphere dominance in children is not usually firmly set until c 7-8 years of age, formal literacy education prior to this is likely to cause difficulties for the 'undecided' child. Some genetic identities may therefore require a later starting point for both the manual dexterity and 'handedness' demanded of most formal literacy programmes.

Two Types of Dyslexia

This study raised the possibility that there could be two forms of disorientation: one purely cognitive/mental and the other affecting whole body/mind integration. In the former, visual and auditory senses are out of synchronisation. This form of disorientation could exist if the literacy programme used was simply incompatible with the child's GI. The idea was previously expressed by both Bushe-Huey (1913) and Clay (1987) that reading problems such as dyslexia are the result of poor teaching. This appears overly harsh, but it is probably the case that the individual child simply cannot find meaning in the code being used. This is because meaning is the result of successful association (integration) of repeated grapheme/phoneme (visual/auditory) stimuli firing simultaneously (G/P/M). Alternatively, as suggested in *Phono-Graphix*, this type of disorientation could also result from too early learning of a system which the child is logically (cognitively) unable to understand, being too young.

A second form of disorientation of a whole body-mind type may result if the individual needs for the child's GI have not been met *prior* to literacy. A pre-existing orientation problem is revealed as the child attempts to map literacy onto an already disorientated sensory system resulting in dyslexic signs. The 2 'Types' are shown below in Fig 12:

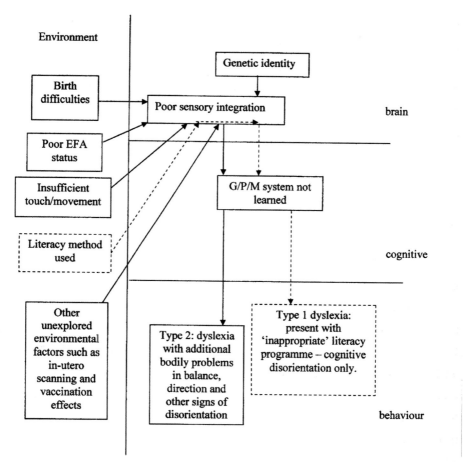

Fig 12. Two 'Types' of Dyslexia

In a child whose body/mind is disorientated but whose GI is compatible with the literary programme used dyspraxic difficulties may occur. The child may require help with these, despite not exhibiting reading problems. Where whole body/mind and cognitive disorientation co-exist it may be preferable to address the body/mind disorientation first in order to ensure all orientation problems have cleared.

The existence of this second body/mind type of dis-orientation can be assessed prior to literacy or in infancy using simple techniques outlined by Goddard (2002) and shown in Chapter 10. If no body/mind disorientation is found, then changing the programme, or waiting until the child is older, would alleviate any purely cognitive 'Type 1' disorientation.

The 'Cause' of Dyslexia

From this research it would appear that 'dyslexia' is different from other learning/ literacy problems. This difference is not to be found in the 'literacy problem' itself, but in the underlying reason/s for the disorientation. This would be why abilities in other areas – except those of orientation or sensory integration – are usually unaffected in children with dyslexia. Clearly, attempting to teach a child to read when the brain-based structures necessary for literacy are not fully integrated will result in the same problems that any child with reading difficulties will show – an inability to read. Except that there will also be additional signs of disorientation, such as those identified by measures of posture or delayed development, as in the DORE or PRI programmes, or the Nicolson and Fawcett Dyslexia Screening Tests. And, in 'whole body' disorientation these signs could remain despite the child learning literacy.

Consequently, it appears entirely correct to suggest that there is a specific literacy problem which can be identified as 'dyslexia'. But that the focus of detection needs to be child rather than brain-based and to be applied prior to literacy education. Unfortunately, because the dominant view of dyslexia is that it is a 'brain problem' and the phonological symptoms of this are the main – if not only – focus, possible ways of helping the child are currently being denied wider application. For example, the DORE programme has received excellent research support (Reynolds, Nicolson and Hambly, 2003). Despite resistance to its implications in some quarters (Elliott, 2005) this research has been well supported (Nicolson 2003) and a variety of PRI exercise-based programmes have also been successfully running within school settings for some time. Rather, it appears to be the inability of phonological theorists to comprehend the connection between the child's 'behaviours' of dyslexia and the underlying structures upon which phonological processing depend which now forms the major obstacle to providing optimum help for children. It is of interest, for example, that Frith's causal model of dyslexia (shown in Chapter 1, Figure 2) allows only for a 'brain' causation and is therefore severely limited. But as this study has suggested, the role of the environment could sometimes be as much as 100% in dyslexia, regardless of genetic brain inheritance.

The ability to perceiving dyslexia as other than a 'brain fault' would appear to be the first step towards knowing what to do about it. The individual sensory problems noticed by different researchers are also likely to remain 'unconnected' unless it is understood that the compound effect of any single sensory difficulty is likely to be disorientation due to poor sensory synchronicity. Equally, if a child is unable to make sense of the code used for literacy, s/he may become cognitively disorientated. Learning to read using a code that allows the child to orientate as they learn (as in multi-sensory teaching or going at the developmental pace of the child) can prevent this.

It would appear from this study that some children are more easily disorientated than others for a variety of reasons which are often essential to their identity. But that most, if not all, can be assisted by adapting the environment to meet their needs. These ideas are discussed further in Chapter 10.

How Successful Programmes for Dyslexia May Work

Having generated a hypothesis using grounded theory it should now be possible to look at any successful programme for dyslexia in the light of the theory of orientation and understand how it 'fits' with the study findings. If there is a programme which cannot be understood to work by bringing about orientation, this would suggest the coding and analysis of the data had been skewed or partial, or the methodology flawed. Alternatively, if other programmes can be seen to act similarly to those in the study this would lend further support to the hypothesis. This section will therefore look at programmes which were not included in the study to find if they too can be accounted for by the hypothesis.

Guy Berard's acoustic method is similar to that of Tomatis, (described in Chapter 2) with whom he trained. Except that Berard does not accept the causative role of the mother in the child's problems. (Modern Tomatis practitioners are also not as judgmental as Tomatis was about the mother's role). As describes in the Tomatis programme, the ear is the centre of 'inner hearing'. Without this 'inner voice' the child cannot really listen. Once 'inner hearing' takes place the sounds of letters can be mapped onto the visual code and integration of both sensory streams can take place. It is also likely that the vestibular (balance) system is under-stimulated where inner hearing is lacking. The vestibular system is itself fundamental to the orientation process. Berard's method therefore appears to act in the same way as that of Tomatis.

The A.R.R.O.W programme, developed by Colin Lane, is another auditory system. A.R.R.O.W stands for: Aural-Read-Respond-Oral-Write. A recording of the learner's own reading voice forms the basis of the programme. This enables the listener to learn to focus on the voice and tune out other distractions in a similar way to *JST, Tomatis and Berard's* methods.

BrightStar is a visual programme which was not included in this study because it was heard of only after the data had been collected. It acts by 'training' the dyslexic person to focus on the details, from the rods of the retina of the eye, and ignore peripheral movements, picked up by the cones. This builds up stronger neuronal connections between the rods and the cerebellum. Over a period of c6 weeks the individual is able to strengthen their visual attention and reduce the intrusion of peripheral visual information. Convergence and attention are increased and distractibility decreased. By strengthening these neural pathways visual information is more able to synchronise with other sensory input during literacy.

Brain Net programmes also work to re-generate neural connections in children with a wide range of developmental disorders or brain damage. Through movement and exercise programmes 'missing' neural connections are stimulated and the child can begin to learn or regain what has been lost. *The Handle Institute* and *A Chance To Grow* have the same aim, but adopt multiple approaches to neural regeneration in their programmes, each of which were covered singly in this study.

Reading Recovery, developed by Marie Clay, is a phonics programme which follows a flexible approach to each child's learning. Specially trained teachers help the child engage in their own learning process concentrating only on what needs to be learned. There is a focus on meaning. Gradually extended literacy strategies are adopted which combine knowledge of how children learn, oral language development in reading, and the reciprocity of reading and writing. *Reading Recovery* has itself been adapted by Peter Hatcher et al (1994) through the addition of multisensory elements, to form the *Cumbria Intervention*.

The *Lindamood ADD* reading programme is similar to *Phono-Graphix* in teaching phonics in a developmentally logical order and was therefore not included.

Phonics programmes work by raising awareness of phonemes – the smallest sounds that make up words. By learning these sounds, and really hearing them, the child can learn to map them onto the visual symbols of letters. Training in the sounds alone will automatically develop neuronal connections for long-term recognition. If these sounds are presented simultaneously with visual symbols, as with multisensory programmes, over time auditory/visual sensory integration and therefore automaticity will occur. As has been seen, the addition of tactile elements enables the child to physically orientate to the visual information by evoking spatial learning through the parietal lobe. The *Hickey Language Course* multisensory programme varies from *Alpha To Omega* in emphasis only. All multisensory programmes share the same synchronising effect on sensory processing enabling orientation to the code.

So, a major point raised by this study's findings is that although apparently diverse programmes all appeared to be doing something different, they actually share the implicit effect of improving orientation through sensory integration. Sometimes they work by developing the neuronal pathways necessary for sensory integration to occur later in literacy (such as *BrightStar, DORE* or *Efalex,* for example) and sometimes they achieve both steps together as in multisensory literacy programmes. Their effects may be purely cognitive or affect the whole body/mind. Successful programmes enable the pathways within and/or between areas of the brain to strengthen, thus enabling the child to gain orientation through sensory synchronicity.

That it is the neural pathways rather than specific brain areas which are affected in dyslexia has been demonstrated by Klingberg et.al (2000). Blakemore and Frith also wonder if:

"Perhaps there are weaker connections between the 3

different regions of the reading system, rather than any specific anatomical abnormalities in the regions themselves." (Blakemore and Frith, 2005, p90)

That the brain develops in response to sensory stimuli has been shown by Tallal (2004). And it is because the brain is 'plastic,' responding to incoming stimuli rather than being fixed like 'hardware,' that programmes are able to act and new learning can take place. Each programme enables this process in its own way. This all-brain sensory effect would help explain why many of the models are effective despite focussing upon different senses. No single sense is actually separate from the others or from the act of creating a meaningful relationship with the perceived environment. Interestingly, it is becoming increasingly apparent that perception is a multisensory act and that regardless of the specific senses involved, the underlying principles which govern perception are multisensory ones (Calvert, Spence & Stein, 2004). It can now also be seen why the more senses involved the better (e.g. by incorporating touch, physical coordination and cross-lateral movement) in order to enable body/mind sensory integration pathways to develop, onto which literacy can then more readily be mapped.

Ron Davis's Orientation Theory

One of the programmes described in Chapter 5 – the Ron Davis Method – adopts the concept of *Orientation Counselling* as part of its programme. In fact, this is the only programme to directly utilise the term *orientation* or address this problem as key in dyslexia. Davis uses the concept to describe the perceptual distortions which occur within a child whose genetic identity is purely visual, believing that dyslexia is the result of the inability to form a meaningful visual image for a word.

Within the orientation theory of dyslexia hypothesis as I suggest it here, this represents a 'Type 1 dyslexia' in a child with a visual genetic identity (GI). And although this is undoubtedly an important part of the problem, it provides only a partial explanation. Davis is quite right in his view that orientation can result from incompatible thinking styles but, as this study suggests, orientation can also take a 'Type 2' body/mind form.

How Orientation Develops

The developmental path of the human has evolved to bring about orientation within a gravitational environment. In the womb, the primitive reflexes and development of the vestibular system prepare the child for the change from aquatic to air-based life. The vestibular is fully myelinated by 5 months after conception and the basic material of the brain has usually developed by about 2 months later. At birth the infant brain is able to process sensory stimuli, a process begun in-utero, and can recognise its mother's and, where present, father's voice and any music that was played frequently before birth (Bremmer, 1994; Hepper, 1991).

Brain development following birth consists almost exclusively of *synaptogenesis*: an explosion of dendrite and synaptic nerve growth which 'wires' together and establishes areas of brain specialisation. Maximum density of around 150% adult level is seen between 4-12 months of age in the infant. This is followed by the 'pruning' of under-utilised brain connections until, by 2 years of age, synaptic density in the infant matches that of adults. The brain is 'moulded' in response to whatever environmental sensory stimulation it receives and humans are extremely shaped by their cultural surroundings. This is because, in order to allow the proportionally large head to pass through the birth passage, human infants are in effect born 'too early'. Consequently, a high percentage of an infant's brain development takes place following birth. Areas such as those to the frontal cortex continue to grow and adjust for between 10-20 years. Brain metabolism (glucose uptake) is also above that of adult levels in the early years peaking at c4-5 years of age.

The brain is 60% fat and, as described in the EFA model in Chapter 6, relies upon DHA (Omega 3) to enable this growth. A rich source of Omega 3 is found in breast-milk, as shown in Table 3 of that programme. Consequently a newborn baby that is breast-fed will automatically receive the essential food necessary to form the development of brain pathways in response to new sensory stimuli. In addition, an infant's rooting and sucking reflexes have evolved to occur instantaneously at birth to enable physical contact with its mother and start to feed.

Brain Specialisation

The infant's brain is extremely 'plastic' and it is crucial to perceive the cortex itself as continually developing from birth onward. In a baby's cortex there are as yet no specialised areas such as those illustrated previously in Fig. 13. And, as Goswami points out:

> "Although adult brains all show this basic structure, it is thought that early in development a number of developmental paths and end states are possible. The fact that development converges on the same basic brain structure across cultures and gene pools is probably to do with the constraints on development present in the environments." (Goswami, 2004, p3)

Specialisation takes place as experience builds up associations, which result in recognition and memory. As this occurs, neuronal connections are made between the appropriate sensory areas to the association areas in the cortex. In a developing brain, where the pathways have not yet been established, any lack of consistent sensory input and/or poor nutrition will necessarily affect the establishment of such pathways.

Movement

It was suggested in the Primary Reflex Inhibition Programme (PRI) described in Chapter 4 that insufficient reflex movements made by infants after birth (primitive reflexes) or as they adjust to a gravitational environment (postural reflexes) will result in these reflexes being retained (Goddard, 2002). However, given ample space and freedom of movement a baby will naturally inhibit each reflex over the time-line shown in Table 2 in the PRI programme. In environments where infants are routinely carried around in a sling or on their mother's back it has been noted that physical orientation is excellent. Rocking is also an automatic response in mothers when holding their babies. Ayres believes:

> "The sensation of gentle body movement tends to organise the brain. – In addition to calming the baby, carrying and rocking provide sensations that are essential building blocks for other sensations and for self-determined body movements." (Ayres, 1991, p17)

The process of maturation is instinctive in human infants and only requires environmental opportunity. Crawling is vital, as described in *Brain Gym* in Chapter 4, because it enables increased development of neuronal connections across the corpus callosum, which unites the left and right hemispheres. Interestingly, Hannaford (1995) of *Brain Gym* suggests lack of visual tracking ability, common in children with literacy problems, may be due to insufficient bodily movement as this strengthens the development of eye muscles. As eye-hand co-ordination replaces the earlier simple tracking of objects the eye will lead the hand-movement, making it possible to connect movement with sight. This is clearly essential for writing, reading and drawing, playing an instrument, sport or dancing. Increased physical interaction with the environment from infancy and as the child grows will therefore enable sufficient multisensory experience to enable orientation.

Touch

Touch is vital at and from birth onwards. The process of birth through the birth canal is crucial for providing the Reticular Activating System (RAS) in the brain stem with the 'wake-up' stimulus necessary to the infant's proprioceptive and vestibular senses. Because these are key to orientation within gravity, infants that lack this birth experience are likely to be at risk of poor sensory orientation of the whole body/mind type. As outlined in Chapter 4, much of the newborn's initial sensory learning is through the skin and action of the primitive reflexes. By the second year s/he can tell where s/he is touched and direct a response voluntarily. Knowledge of the physical body enables awareness within gravity and therefore orientation. However, un-integrated sensations from the skin will prevent spatial awareness leading to trouble learning to do buttons and zippers, for example, and the child may become dyspraxic and/or frequently drop things. As Ayres (1991) states:

"The ability to plan movements depends upon the accuracy of the child's touch system" (p8).

Visual Convergence

The first 2 years of an infant's life are crucial for visual integration. In the Magnocellular Theory in Chapter 3, Stein in particular stresses the centrality of binocular focus and convergence. Visual convergence is crucial to enable meaningful grapheme/phoneme (visual/auditory) mapping during literacy and was found to be very weak in Stein's dyslexic groups. The human infant has evolved to visually converge on its mother's face through gaze during holding and breast-feeding. Innately a newborn baby displays a preference for faces and in particular for the mother's face (Field et.al 1982) smell and voice (DeCasper & Fifer, 1980). One immediate interaction that proceeds between the mother and newborn child is mother-to-child eye contact. Klaus, Kennell and Klaus (1995) observed that mothers alone with their infants shortly after birth show a strong interest in eye-to-eye contact. Several expressed the view that once the infant had looked at them they felt closer to him/her. Parents showed a remarkable increase (from 10% to 23%) in the time spent in the *en face* position – parent and infant face-to-face with their heads aligned in the same parallel plane – from the first to fifth minute after birth.

A newborn baby mature at birth (i.e. not premature) can see clearly but has a short range of focus which will converge at about 8-10 inches (20-25cm). This is the distance which separates the infant's face from its mother's when the baby is held or breast-fed. Each time the child looks at the face the multisensory neural pathways for convergence will 'fire' and the connections become stronger. The child is more likely to gaze at the face if spoken to by that person (Bremmer 1994) thus increasing auditory/visual multisensory firing associations. Convergence, if it is not exact at birth, will therefore establish as the child is frequently held, fed and talked to, while eye contact is made, with or without additional visual stimulation.

Motherese

Human mothers (and most adults) automatically adopt a form of speech with infants known as *Motherese* which appears to be universal and cross-cultural. According to Gopnik, Meltzoff and Kuhl (1999):

> "Motherese sentences are shorter and simpler than sentences directed at adults. Moreover, grown-ups talking to babies often repeat the same thing over and over with slight variations. – these characteristics of Motherese may help children to figure out the words and grammar of their language. – Recent studies have shown that the well-formed, elongated consonants and vowels of Motherese are particularly clear examples of speech sounds." (p130)

Babies given a choice of sounds chose to hear mothers talking to infants in Motherese in preference to mothers talking to other adults. They chose Motherese regardless of language or when the words had been filtered out using computer techniques to give only the pitch of the voice. Gopnik, Meltzoff and Kuhl appear surprised to note:

> "– Motherese seems to actually help babies solve the language problem." (Gopnik, Meltzoff and Kuhl 1999, p130)

But, not only is this the case but it also instigates the important 1:1 to-and-fro-rhythmic 'conversation' between mother and baby. This is the *intersubjectivity,* described in the Music-Making programme in Chapter 5, which precedes and underlies formal speech. It is the basis of language and social communication and the foundation of 'beat detection' (Goswami 2003, p465). Merzenich (1993) too describes how mother/child interaction can help 'practice discrimination' between phonemes. This is important, because there is some evidence that a precursor to the phonological difficulties in dyslexia is vocabulary and expressive language skill. As Mutter states:

> "Deficits in language skill at ages 2-4 may reflect underlying problems in linguistic precursors of phonological awareness." (Mutter, 2003, p109)

If as Mutter suggests speech and language use is a predictor of later reading ability quality of Motherese is clearly extremely relevant. Without Motherese children do not receive the necessary auditory (and probably vestibular) stimulation they require. Yet, Savan (2000) found, 80% of children with special needs in literacy had not received sufficient high frequency auditory stimulation during the first two years of life for a variety of reasons. She has also proposed that orientation can be affected by this lack. As the inferior parietal lobe of the cortex receives input from the RAS, thalamus and auditory association areas, this appears very likely.

Hart and Risley (1995) found that Motherese varied according to socio-economic group. Mothers in a 'professional' group used a more complex sentence structure, a richer vocabulary and a highly affirmative feedback style whereas 'welfare' mothers often used a negative tone and more disapproval. They did not differ in any other measure such as affection, concern for the child or cleanliness of the home. Nor was race a factor in the study. By age 3 it was estimated that children in the 'professional' grouping had heard nearly 35 million words, the 'middle-class' children just over 20 million and the 'welfare' group around 10 million words. These differences were found even though 'welfare' mothers spent on average more time with their children.

Overall the various measures of the mother's speech taken together were highly correlated to the child's later language skills including to standardised measures of IQ and language use. These correlations were much more powerful when based on parenting speech style rather than socio-economic group measured at aged 3 and aged 9, varying between .74 and .82. To avoid difficulties it would appear sensible to postpone formal literacy until the child had resolved handedness when s/he would have become fully orientated. Macrae (1998) reports that doing so enables children to learn literacy extremely quickly and with better results than those who had started 2 years earlier.

Breast Feeding

In addition to the nutritional and health benefits of breast-milk, described in the *Efalex* programme in Chapter 4, the act of breast-feeding provides increased opportunities for multi-sensory stimulation through mother/child bonding, handling and touching of the infant, visual convergence, pre-lingual communication, 'rapport' and high-pitched auditory stimulation established through Motherese. In fact, taken as a whole it can be seen that the mother is acting as a 'Matrix' for the infant's orientation into the gravitational world. Schore suggests:

> "She (mother) acts as the primary facilitator in the early months for the formation of connections between different levels in the brain and the laying of foundations not only for later learning ability but also for emotional functioning and immune response." (In Goddard, 2002, p136)

Diamond et al (1963) also describes the mother as:

> "– playing the role of higher brain structures: she is the child's auxiliary cortex."

Sanger and Kelly describe this as an 'ontological adaption' in which a robust burst of growth occurs when an environment attains a perfect pitch of harmony (rapport) with the needs of the organism it is supporting (Sanger & Kelly, 1985). They refer to the maternal matrix as *'The Magic Square'* to represent this evolutionary development. The quality of 'the fit' between mother and child is therefore considered essential in enabling optimum infant development. It can be seen that the 'Mother as Matrix' is the means by which the human species has evolved to allow orientation of the new infant human into the multi-sensory, gravitational world.

The WHO (Newman, 1995) recommendation to breast-feed a baby for at least 2 years is therefore extremely important if the sensory pathways (including the magnocellular highway of the thalamus) are to adequately support this development. Sucking also stimulates the bonding chemical (oxytocin) in the mother which ensures the infant's survival and decreases the likelihood of the mother abandoning her child.

The Evolution of Orientation

The way humans have evolved to bring about orientation is though interactive newborn multisensory communion with their mothers/caretakers: A newborn child will receive high-frequency auditory stimulation; the right nutrition for the developing brain and proprioceptive/vestibular stimulus to the parietal lobe (the orientating lobe) simply by being born naturally, breast-fed, talked to and held, at and after birth. Through natural movements made by the infant the primary and postural reflexes enable the child to develop from a water to an air environment and from prone to upright to enable orientation within gravity. In this process, the mother acts as a 'matrix' until the infant is c.7 years of age and has fully orientated to the gravitational environment, as signalled by the establishment of handedness. At this stage s/he is physically independent of the mother. But if, as is the suggested hypothesis of this study, disorientation is at the core of dyslexia, and/or if some of the developmental elements are lacking, so that a child has become disorientated, the question remains: What can be done to bring about orientation? This question is explored fully in the final chapter where I present a 'Positive Manifesto' for dyslexia.

CHAPTER 10

A POSITIVE MANIFESTO FOR DYSLEXIA

As described in the *Introduction*, when I first started this research project I had no prior experience or knowledge of dyslexia. Adopting a *grounded theory* methodology enabled me to bring an overview to the field and search for what might be common in successful programmes. I found a wide and apparently diverse range of successful programmes available. Several of these were non-literary and some were not part of established practice, but on the basis of children's own experiences that these programmes had helped them, I decided to include them in the study. One of the benefits of the grounded theory approach is that it can generate new insights, or hypotheses. It is therefore possible to use it as a bridge between quantative (statistical) and qualitative (experiential) data.

It is also in the nature of grounded theory to return to the original data/research sources with each new insight that is gained. In this way it was discovered that the theory of *sensory integration* (described in Chapter 9) is not new but had become eclipsed in recent decades by a focus on the purely mental (cognitive) aspects of dyslexia rather than on the whole child. Likewise, I found a rich body of activity and thought on teaching to children's differences, which has remained relatively outside mainstream educational policy. In the final chapter I refer to this and, using the hypothesis of orientation theory as a guiding principle, construct a 'positive manifesto' for helping the child with dyslexia: the first element of which is to establish which 'type' of disorientation the child is experiencing before deciding upon the best approach for teaching literacy.

Establishing Which 'Type' of Dyslexia

This study generated the idea that there may be two 'types' of dyslexia. Looking at the literature again, it can be seen that many attempts have been made to understand the variety of sensory difficulties within dyslexia. Stein (2001) for example, notes 3 different types: visual, auditory and a combination of both, but believes auditory forms share the same underlying causation as the visual form through the magnocellular system. Sally Goddard of the INPP primary reflex inhibition programme identifies 4 categories:

a)   problems with accurate decoding and processing of visual information

b)   phonological processing problems

c)   families in which there is a strong genetic tendency

d)   motor-perceptual and vestibular related functions

Of these she considers the 4th responds best to an exercise-based programme (Goddard, 2006). In contrast this study suggests only two 'types' of dyslexia, which contain the other types. Type 1 would account for many forms of a) and b) of the above categories and Type 2 for a) and b) where d) was also present. c) – a family history of different thinking styles (GIs) – could lead to cases in both groups.

Clearly, if the underlying developmental needs of children have not been met, orientation will probably not take place and visual and auditory integration problems will occur. Addressing the underlying developmental needs of the child might resolve all forms and/or make it plain that the child required a learning programme compatible with their GI. Any child who does not understand, or is too young to make sense of the code, will obviously struggle with literacy. Therefore, understanding the 'type' of dyslexia will provide the 'reason' for the learning problem, indicating the best way to resolve it. (A range of resources for the steps described in this *Manifesto* are given in appendix IV)

Genetic Identity and Learning Style

As described in Chapter 9, this study generated the concept of *genetic identity* as a route out of pathologising children who might think differently. Similar concepts reflecting differences in thinking style can be found. *Learning styles*, *cognitive styles*, Hannaford's *dominance profiles* and the concept of *Multiple Intelligences* (Gardiner, 1983) have been gaining popularity in educational practice for some time. However, as is usually the case, there is a great deal of debate about exactly what a 'learning style' is and the differences between these terms. Mortimore, in reviewing a variety of approaches, concludes:

1.   *Cognitive style* is an individual's characteristic and relatively consistent way of processing incoming information from the environment.

2.   A student's *learning style* describes the strategies used in a learning situation. (Mortimore, 2006 p8)

These descriptions could equally reflect the thinking of an orientated as a disorientated child. A *genetic identity* (GI) has something in common with Gardiner's concept of *multiple intelligences* in which different forms of intelligence are proposed. For example, Gardiner suggests there are linguistic; logico-mathematical; bodily/kinaesthetic; social; musical; spatial, and personal (to do with relationships and feelings) forms of intelligence. He proposes these are partly genetic, but also require for their expression the environmental and cultural influences which allow them to develop. GI is also similar to the notion of *thinking styles* which Sternberg (1997) believes describe the preferred way of using our abilities. Hannaford's *dominance profiles* are probably the most wide-ranging in identifying the actual brain wiring patterns of children (and adults). She states:

> "Over the years – I observed a discouraging incongruity between the school teaching practices and the learning styles of a majority of students. In general schools expect students to learn in a certain way and the students who do not fit this type are often viewed as inferior instead of merely as different learners." (Hannaford, 1997, p11-12)

As described in the *Brain Gym* programme in Chapter 4, she gives 32 different combinations of brain/ear/eye/hand/foot laterality. Her guide includes how to determine an individual profile plus the strengths and weaknesses of each.

Distinguishing Developmental Needs from a GI

It is clearly important to separate developmental needs, delays or damage, which may be expressed through differing learning styles, from genetic identity itself. This is because children whose learning styles reflect lacks in their environmental needs or development (Type 2 dyslexias) may require different sorts of help from 'different thinkers' (Type 1). Their adopted learning style may be masking developmental or identity needs. For example, a child who is uncertain about handedness may have been rushed to elect a preference due to the need for formal literacy at aged 4. This may have set up a particular 'wiring' which is not entirely in tune with the natural GI of the child. If, for example, literacy had been delayed, as it is in many Continental European countries, the child may have settled on their own preferred 'wiring' at a later date – usually by aged 8/9.

The effects of delayed development, as in retained reflexes, can also masquerade as learning styles. For example, McPhillips (2001) found insufficient children without a retained Asymmetrical Tonic Neck Reflex (ATNR) to form a separate group for his study. These are not genetic identities. These are developmental problems of a 'Type 2' disorientation which need to be addressed, especially prior to literacy. Therefore, despite the excellent progress being made in teaching to learning styles, it is important to ensure that they are the elected preference of the child and not a compensatory pattern for developmental problems.

A non-compensatory learning style – in keeping with the child's GI – is more likely to express itself as simple 'Type 1'dyslexia without additional co-ordination problems or reflex retention. This is because, whereas language does appear to be innate and we were all born pre-programmed to make the sounds our ancestors made and to fit into any language anywhere at birth, the same is not true for literacy. There is no innate literacy programme in the human child. An arbitrarily chosen 'code' was devised which each child is now required to learn. Provided a child hears all the phonemes (tiny sounds) that make up the words, they can learn the code. But the code has to be 'cracked'. It doesn't necessarily flow from phoneme awareness.

Those genetic identities in tune with whoever originally designed the code will therefore probably grasp it more quickly than those who would have chosen a different communication system. It is also important to remember, as Blakemore and Frith (2005, p72) suggest, that literacy alters the wiring in the brain leading to compensatory brain wiring similar to a form of 'brainwashing'. Leslie Hart's research has also shown that the whole curriculum must be 'brain-compatible' or it cannot be learned (Winebrenner, 1996, p42). If children are not given learning tasks compatible with their brain style they will become stressed, which triggers the 'fight or flight' mechanism in the brain stem, preventing full attention and interfering with learning. As Hannaford suggests in the *Brain Gym* programme, described in Chapter 4, excess stress can interfere with dominance patterns. Johansen of JST (Chapter 2) has also noticed that ear dominance in children can change in overly loud environments.

On this basis, of the 3 chromosome associations with dyslexia, noted in the *Efalex* programme described in Chapter 7, there would be two genetic identities (C2 and C15) and one compensatory learning style (C6). Whilst C2 is associated with left-handedness (Bishop 2004) which has been found to be common in dyslexic children, it is definitely not pathological. And it is my suggestion that C15 is probably connected with naturally visual thinkers who have more developed parvocellular pathways and connect up apparently unconnected elements to form new 'patterns', ideas and solutions. These are both part of the child's identity.

The C6 connection however could come about due to reduced brain-nutrition, or vaccine/illness-induced inflammations in the presence of under-nourishment with essential fatty acids. Stein, for example, cites changes to the major histocompatibility complex (MHC) Class I region on the short arm of Chromosome 6 (Stein, 2001, p28). This is involved with immunological regulation and the lack of essential polyunsaturated fatty acids (PUFAs). Immune reactions mobilise PUFAs in order to provide the precursors of the cytokines required for effective response to foreign agents. Dyslexia is associated with low essential fatty acids which weaken the immune system. And while the teaching of these children would still be to their preferred learning style and dominance profile, it is important that we recognise compensatory learning styles so that the causes of damage in, for example C6, can be rectified and/or prevented with future children, and the needs of those who are left-handed or visual thinkers (for example) are legitimised and more readily met within their normal lives.

Establishing a Child's Genetic Identity

The first step to establishing a true GI is therefore to distinguish the type of disorientation the child is experiencing and to separate out any developmental compensation. This can be done using the following methods: (A) detecting the presence of retained primitive/postural reflexes and/or disorientation and (B) determining the child's *dominance profile*. As described it is best to do these in this order so as to remove any compensatory learning styles due to disorientation problems before choosing a teaching method optimum for the child

A   Retained Reflexes

Retained primitive reflexes provide an early sign that a child has orientation problems (see Chapter 4, PRI programme for a full description). The ATNR, which is inhibited at c6 months when the child begins cross-crawling, if retained beyond this, is also an indicator for the likely retention of other reflexes. It is frequently present in children with dyslexia. Goddard describes how to test for this, and the other reflexes, in a child:

Test Position

Standing, feet together, with the arms held straight out at shoulder level and height, but with the hands relaxed at the wrists.

Procedure

Tester stands behind the subject and gives the instruction: "When I turn your head, I want you to keep your arms straight out in front of you, as they are now. This means your arms remain in the same position and only your head moves." Tester then slowly rotates the subject's head until the chin is parallel with the shoulder. Pause for 10 seconds. Return the head to the midline. Pause for 10 seconds. Rotate the head to the other side and pause for 10 seconds. Repeat the procedure up to 4 times.

Observations

Any movement of the hand and arm on the side to which the head is turned, i.e. do the arms automatically follow the movements of the head?

Scoring

0   no response
1   slight movement of the arms in the direction the face is pointed
2   movement of the arms in the direction of the head to 45 degrees
3   arm movement to 60 degrees or flexion of the opposite side
4   90 degrees of the arms and/or loss of balance as a result of head rotation

Depending upon the score, as given above, Goddard advises seeking help for the child individually at a treatment centre. Or, for those with a lower degree of retention (indicated by a lower score) through a group movement programme (Goddard 2002, p86). There are also several

Brain Gym moves which will inhibit this reflex, which can be found through the *Brain Gym* organisation.

The presence of the later postural reflexes which are usually related to cerebellar and vestibular problems in the older child, can be found through tests for cerebellar involvement, such as Nicolson and Fawcett (1996/2004) *Dyslexia Screening Test* (DST and PREST) the latter being suitable for children of 4 years upwards. These will highlight disorientation problems of Type 2. Although parents can access these later tests themselves through programmes such as PRI, DORE/DDAT or *Brain-Gym*, these cannot yet be accessed freely. Nor do they yet form part of all dyslexia screening assessments (for example the Dyslexia Institute does not offer the coordination elements of testing). However, it is entirely possible for these sorts of programmes to be incorporated into normal school activities.

School-Based Developmental Programmes
Although Goddard suggests how to test and treat retained reflexes, it is actually not easy for parents to access help for these problems outside of private treatment programmes. As an alternative, it would be a simple matter for every child to be assessed for retained ATNR and/or Tonic Labyrinthine Neck Reflex (TLR) by the equivalent of a school nurse or welfare officer. In addition, any of the already successful programmes for remediating cerebellar and vestibular problems could be built into the curriculum as part of their school gym programmes. This is already the case in several schools. For example, Blythe and Goddard have developed – and are currently running – training programmes for teachers to incorporate reflex inhibition exercise programmes into schools. In Chester, the cost of a day's teaching in how to implement the programme is currently £105 plus VAT. This enables the teacher to start using the programme with a whole class of children. For Local Education Authorities (LEAs) training costs £1000 plus VAT, but up to

40 teachers from different schools in the LEA area can attend making this inexpensive and accessible for wide areas. The programme devised (The INPP Test Battery and Developmental Movement Programme For use in Schools) has been taught throughout the UK, Germany and the Netherlands and has been supported by published research and small-scale independent studies (Goddard, 2005). But, because of the current conviction among many within the dyslexia research field, that only the mental/ cognitive elements of dyslexia are relevant and the underlying causation is 'not part of the problem', this sort of work is not being made as available as it could be.

Goddard found 100% of a sample of 54 children with dyslexia had a retained ATNR and TLR and about 50% showed cerebellar involvement. This is interesting as it suggests cerebellar involvement may be a secondary effect in some children of the underlying delayed development of retained primitive reflexes. Work studying the connection between cerebellar/vestibular functioning, postural reflexes and the underlying connection with dyslexia has been undertaken since the 1970s. This is the approach utilised in the DORE/DDAT method, although deQuiros and Schraeger, Kohen-Raz and Levinson, Blythe and McGowen and the Belgaus have all provided evidence of this connection prior to this programme (Goddard, 2006). The DORE/DDAT method addresses balance and coordination using developmentally later exercises (postural rather than primitive reflexes) whereas PRI programmes also provides the earlier developmental 'entry point' (primitive reflexes):

"The former programme is appropriate where the later postural reflexes are implicated, and will improve strength and coordination in all cases, but where there are retained primitive (earlier) reflexes it is necessary to go to the deeper ones." (Goddard, 2006)

And, although the DORE/DDAT method is not 'new' it is an example of an independent individual re-discovering the role of the cerebellum because of its lack of prominence in established approaches to dyslexia. This occurred when Winfred Dore's own daughter attempted suicide because there was no effective help being offered for her dyslexia. It has been known for 30 years that many cases of dyslexia are sensory-based and yet parents and educational policy makers have both been denied access to this knowledge and practical options based on this research. There is still considerable and quite unnecessary hostility shown towards programmes which are non-literary (Elliott, 2005).

One cannot help but ask why there is so much antagonism towards non-literary programmes? It is certainly not because they do not work, lack research support or mislead the public, as none of these are true. On the contrary they appear to have been extremely helpful to many children and are easy and cost effective to incorporate into schools. And although no one would wish to make money from children's problems, this is after all only what commercial drug companies are both permitted and expected to do. Exercise programmes to rectify developmental delays in children could become part of educational policy, removing the need for parents to find assessments and expensive treatment for their children outside of their learning environment. The best time, however, for developmental delays or in-coordination problems to be highlighted is prior to literacy acquisition as part of Early Years nursery education programmes. This is explored later in the chapter.

B   Identifying the Child's Dominance Profile

A child's dominance profile can be determined using the simple instructions given by Hannaford (1997) which will establish which hand, foot, ear and eye is dominant (left or right for each) and marking this information on a chart. Hannaford describes the likely strengths and difficulties of all 32 dominance profile combinations, including compensatory effects under stress. For example, auditory able learners have their dominant ear opposite their dominant brain hemisphere (regardless of which hemisphere this is) and prefer auditory presentation when learning new information. If the dominant ear is on the same side as the dominant hemisphere (an *auditory limited profile*) auditory access is decreased under stress and learning through listening may prove difficult. Hannaford's research suggests that over half of all learners have this latter pattern, and yet the majority of teaching is verbal (Hannaford, 1997, p27-8). Once any compensatory patterns have been identified and treated, and using Hannaford's guide for parents and teachers, the child's profile can be identified and learning needs highlighted. This process could be undertaken in schools as part of the initial entry procedure and/or at any time during the child's early development.

A Note on Gender Differences and GI

It is important to emphasise that GIs are not gender specific. Although it is popular to find books stating there are brain-based differences between the sexes, knowing as we do that the brains of babies are plastic, it is becoming harder to make any claims for a hard-wired thinking difference between the genders. However, it is thought that boys tend to have more development in certain areas of the right hemisphere, which gives them increased spatial abilities such as required in mechanical design, and that girls have better language and communication skills. Interestingly, the developmental step from right-hemisphere to left hemisphere (noted by Tomatis and Bakker in Chapter 2) which takes place in infants, commences later in males than females making boys particularly susceptible to problems from early formal literacy.

There seems to be some evidence too that boys are delayed in their overall development by c.2 years compared with girls and that they like to move more when they learn (or are more restless with passive learning) due to lower serotonin levels. Boys tend to spread out and take space from girls if sharing a space, possibly for this reason although it was not clear if they did this when sharing with other boys. Consequently, teaching boys and girls together requires consideration for the needs of both genders. Gurian (2001) provides detailed research and practical information on this. In general, a child joining formal schooling is currently required to move from a movement/ tactile-based environment to a language-based, relatively physically static one. This may inadvertently cause any child with a movement GI – considerable problems. In addition, and quite apart from gender, movement is important in enabling the increased employment of thinking strategies, increased understanding of self in relation to others and to space, and increased ability to interact with others (Zaichkowsky, Zaichkowsky & Martinek, 1980, p11). These are all good reasons therefore to incorporate movement into learning in schools.

Environmental Factors

In Olson's (2004) twin research, cited in Chapter 1, it was found that only 50% of his sample showed an inherited factor in their reading problem (the child's GI). The other 50% was connected to environmental factors which predisposed them to difficulty with the programme they were given to learn. Environmental factors include nutrition, parenting skills and beliefs and cultural attitudes to literacy including education policies and social policies concerning children. Olson also found that this environmental 50% was capable of diminishing the relevance of the inherited factor sometimes completely. In other words, with the right environmental input, a child's genetic type may be irrelevant in problems of literacy. This suggests that by arranging the environment to give the child what they need it is possible for any GI to gain literacy with no problems. This applies directly to the teaching methods used.

Compatible Teaching

Once any underlying disorientation or developmental delay is highlighted and remedied, and the child's likely genetic identity identified, the optimum literacy programme for the child can be found. The need is to find the programme to suit the child, and not vice versa as is traditionally the case. The way a child processes information is part of their identity and must be taken into account when we teach. Rather than a 'transmission' process in education, as Reid points out:

> "It is the role and the responsibilities of the education system, the school and the individual teacher to ensure that these differences are catered for within the system. This is a tall order and perhaps an idealistic desire, but the key point is that it represents an attitude shift and such a shift is necessary if teachers are to be able to accommodate to the range of differences within most classrooms today" (Reid, 2005, p17).

Clearly different teaching models are required to meet this aim. Reid (2005) provides an excellent resource for these and Winebrenner (1996) a wealth of material covering all aspects of teaching to a child's learning style. Gardner's *multiple intelligences* concept has stimulated an enormous amount of readily accessible child and teacher friendly teaching material. Mortimore's (2006) guide focuses specifically on children with dyslexia and also contains an extensive resource section. (Full details are given at the end of this chapter.)

Whole-School Teaching

An economical and inclusive approach is to adopt a teaching method which *all* children can understand. 'Whole-school' teaching is:

> "aimed at developing appropriate educational strategies for a wide range of learners with different aptitudes and achievements" (Reason, 2001, p300).

An example can be found in the British Dyslexia Association's (BDA's) *Dyslexia Friendly School* guidance. The British Government has supported this scheme, for example in Wales. Their guidance suggests:

> "The skills and strategies which dyslexic children need in order to learn can be taught. And what is good for the dyslexic learner is good for everyone – more children are successful when taught using dyslexia friendly methods – and while dyslexia friendly techniques can be applied to children who are not dyslexic, this does not work the other way around" (BDA/DfEE, 1998).

Full details of the *Dyslexia Friendly Schools* guidance is available on the BDA website whose address is supplied at the end of this chapter. Again it is hard to understand why this approach is not being adopted on a wide scale especially as there is nothing revolutionary about the method adopted – which is multisensory teaching. As mentioned earlier, phonics programmes (now the UK Government's preferred strategy) are made much more effective by the addition of multisensory elements (for example the *Cumbria Intervention*). Phonics in itself is not sufficient for many children with reading problems. This is because they cannot physically orientate to them. It may simply be that children who find problems with literacy have a greater need for visual systems, tactile systems or movement, for example, due to their GIs. And by using multisensory methods they are better able to orientate themselves to the code.

It might also be that literacy is not 'natural' for them, in that the areas needed to integrate concepts together are more 'spread out' than in other brains. For example, a movement or kinaesthetic (tactile) person could find the 'up and down' concept difficult unless s/he can connect it with real movement (tracing in the air, jumping and crouching or singing high and low). Programmes such as the *Cumbria Intervention*, which add multisensory elements to a phonics base; *Phono-Graphix* and the *Lindamood Reading Programme*, which explain the code in a way that children can understand; Ron Davis's method, developed specifically for visual thinkers; and *Alpha-to Omega*, which returns the child to a 'younger age' as well as adopting a multisensory approach, appear to enable the child to hear the sounds and learn the symbols for them much better than many other phonics programmes. An alternative way to help children avoid literacy problems, other than to identify their preferred thinking style, would be to address their developmental needs fully prior to literacy.

Early Years Education

A child does not fully develop their brain dominance and orientate fully until about 7-9 years of age, depending upon the individual child. The nursery years from aged 4-7 can therefore be seen as a continuation of the development of orientation. It was mentioned earlier that some Continental European school practices delay formal literacy teaching until c 7/8 years and spend the first part of school preparing the child both for literacy and for learning. These practices are well established, and have been found to give better SATS test results after 6 weeks tuition (using the British tests translated into different languages) for those children, than for British children who had received *2 years more* formal literacy teaching (Macrae, 1998). The activities these children were given prior to formal literacy education included verbal skills (describing hidden items to other children) playing games with letter and name sounds; dancing and making shapes of letters in the air or sand; becoming comfortable with group activities, singing and music-making and semi-structured games where the children devised the story and action while the teachers supported.

The nursery staff in these countries were shocked that British children are force-fed literacy as young as 4 years old considering it harmful to attempt formal reading or writing until the child had developed sufficiently to be able to undertake it. (Macrae clearly demonstrates the distress of a 4-year old boy in a British Primary School, unable to hold his pencil but expected to learn to write). Similar multisensory practices are also found in the Steiner/Waldorf educational programmes where formal literacy is delayed until 7 years and eurythmy and art-making is considered important. It is interesting too that there are 'predictors of dyslexia' which depend upon just the skills that are being taught in these European nursery educational programmes.

Language Development as a 'Predictor' of Dyslexia

Apart from the presence of retained reflexes (the ANTR and TRL in particular) and balance and coordination problems, which can be highlighted by tests such as Nicolson and Fawcett's (1996) '*Wobble test*' or Schrager's (2001) '*One-Leg Stand Test*' a major developmental signpost which can act as a 'predictors' of later dyslexia is poor vocabulary growth and mean length of utterance (MLU). MLU – the measure of the complexity of a child's speech – is found to be lower in many children with dyslexia. Bishop and Adams (1990) believe MLU to be:

> . 'The strongest and most consistent 4.5 year old predictor of
> subsequent reading ability.' (p1041)

The style and complexity of speech between mothers and children correlates with their vocabulary development and this is found to be highly relevant to later phoneme-awareness. In Hart and Risley's research (described in Chapter 9) for example, the speed and style of the mother's speech was more significant than her socio-economic status.

Given this, and the other 'predictors' of a child's potential developmental readiness for literacy, any activity that stimulates speech, concepts within language, listening and rhythm, prior to literacy is therefore of great value in preparing the child for formal literacy education. Familiarisation with sounds and their meanings, shapes and characteristics is one of the fundamental aspects of current European early years education. It is also one way of providing a level playing field for children of different socio-economic groups, and/or highlighting those who may not have completely adequate phoneme recognition, for whatever reason prior to formal literacy acquisition. Consequently, there is a real case for adopting the multisensory language-based early years education of other European countries and extending the pre-literacy years. All the signs are that this will avoid children – especially boys – failing at literacy by ensuring they are able to learn it easily when developmentally ready.

The Extended Matrix

In Chapter 9, I outlined how orientation has evolved to come about through the mother/child relationship. In this the mother acts as the 'matrix' or framework through and within which the infant develops from a water to a gravity/air based environment. Because the child does not develop full orientation until about 7 years of age, usually marked by the establishment of handedness in line with their GI, any nursery education becomes the child's extended 'matrix' and must operate with the awareness that they substitute for the child's mother at this time. This would mean operating with a focus on enabling the development of the whole child, rather than purely their education. Practices such as those so clearly effective in Continental European nursery education, do just this. Only with the adoption of their chosen handedness would formal literacy begin. According to current research this is quickly acquired if physical orientation is established prior to literacy.

Orientation Theory and the Dyslexia 'Debate'

There have always been those who have questioned whether dyslexia is a discreet problem, requiring a specific 'diagnosis'. In particular, a review of research by Stanovich (1994) found that a dyslexic group could not be distinguished from the normal continuum of poor reading on any sub-skills. And Long (2000) cites Fletcher and colleagues (1994) that phonological awareness was the main characteristic of all types of reading problem in their study. Dyslexia is often considered a discrete reading problem because in its assessment the general intelligence of the child is taken into account noting a 'discrepancy' between their general ability and that in literacy. However, as children of low educational intelligence can be taught to read, and the discrepancy test does not allow for children with lower overall intelligence who may nevertheless be 'dyslexic,' this criterion appears unsatisfactory. Recently, Elliott (2005) has once again challenged the discreet existence of dyslexia, being critical of what he perceives as a trap into which parents and teachers fall when treating some children with literacy problems differently on the basis of no observable literary measure. He believes it is unhelpful to focus on a singled out elite identified as dyslexic, seeing this as the retreat of the 'middle classes' in the face of their child's illiteracy.

Orientation Theory can lend much to clarifying this debate in suggesting that some children are unable to process the symbols (code) being used to represent language. This is not a matter of intelligence, but of perception due either to an underlying sensory integration problem, or to confusion by the code being used. As previously outlined, there will be a variety of factors which will affect literacy acquisition. A child whose early language has failed to establish the phoneme sounds of English will not recognise these sounds in literacy. An Early Years programme aimed at establishing language awareness and sub-skills prior to formal literacy will ensure this disadvantage is eliminated on a child-by-child basis. A child whose sensory integration – for whatever reason – has been partial, will experience no associative mapping of sound and symbol until those associations are made explicit and integration can become established. Likewise, a child whose Genetic Identity requires visual or kinaesthetic expression of ideas, will struggle with the English orthography.

But, by adopting the *Manifest* – or a similar approach – as outlined in this chapter, the current difficulties raised by Elliott and others are removed because each child's developmental and learning needs *must* be assessed prior to literacy. Whereas 'Type 1' children, and those with no body/mind disorientation, will benefit simply from ways to help them understand the code, children with 'Type 2' problems require help to become fully physically orientated first and may or may not then require the same help in acquiring the code as the cognitively 'confused' group (Type 1). At heart Elliott's is a call for equality and an end to an unequal system of help-provision, as he perceives it. The situation he describes results largely from the current difficulty of the phonological core deficit theory to fully explain dyslexia. By understanding the wider problems it becomes much clearer what needs to be done to help all children, and that these problems can be remedied without a 'diagnosis' of dyslexia as currently understood and without the 'failure' necessary before help can be sought. *Orientation Theory* levels the socio-economic playing field in the way Elliot and others desire, by accepting that dyslexia is connected to the specific developmental and learning needs of individual children, which requires a different way of helping them to acquire literacy. Finally, it must be pointed out that the manifesto is in itself an inclusive policy for helping all children which is pre-emptive and avoids either singling out unfortunate children, or waiting until they 'fail' before offering hard-to-come-by remedial assistance.

Criticism of the Study

As is usual with any piece of research, criticisms will be made. All grounded theory is a personal venture and this one is no exception offering as it does an attempted overview of the entire field of dyslexia research and practice. There are however two reasons for confidence in the results. One is that the study actually found something common across all successful programmes. This is in itself remarkable if we are to accept, as most do, that many of these programmes are 'fads' or offering 'false hopes', or part of a collective delusion of dyslexic families – as they are habitually portrayed. On the contrary, it appears that however different the programmes may seem superficially, and regardless of the way in which they may be accounted for by their proponents, in practice all appeared to work by assisting in orientating the child's sensory perceptions.

The second reason for confidence is that the hypothesis is not entirely new. As described in Chapter 1, there are already theorists working towards an understanding of the underlying causes of dyslexia (for example Nicolson and Fawcett's cerebellar and Stein's magnocellular theories). This study is only an extension of their work and, importantly, that of Herbert Birch in the early 1960s. His sensory integration theory was abandoned with the growing cognitive revolution within psychology, in which the brain became the focus at the expense of the rest of the person. This has led to the current over-emphasis on disassociated brain function, and to a failure to see phoneme awareness as a symptom and not necessarily the 'cause' of dyslexia. *Orientation Theory* also provides a more satisfactory explanation for why multisensory teaching is effective, something lacking at present, as there is no theory of why sensory integration is important to support its teaching. If the hypothesis had been completely new it would carry less weight. As it is, *Orientation Theory* simply connects multiple strands from the existing body of research and presents them in a new way to suggest a theory of dyslexia which is both logical and in tune with the developmental needs of the child. It is a truly developmental theory of developmental dyslexia. That it is challenging to some, is part of the purpose of science.

It is my assertion that a major obstacle facing scientific progress is the apparent inability of many to allow creative thought without perceiving it as a threat. In this, the field of dyslexia is no different from any other human activity when ego is permitted to colour reason. *Decoding Dyslexia* represents a quest to pursue the reality of dyslexia programmes in a way more open to true scientific discovery. There will always be those who dismiss research simply because the findings don't fit with their current understanding (believing we have to understand everything we discover before its existence can be accepted) or because they just don't like the result. I have found this latter attitude: 'It can't be true because I don't want it to be' to be more common in science than is generally supposed. But it represents a mental constraint which impedes further knowledge and the application of available solutions. This is despite the fact that these solutions already exist, as this research has shown. It is only necessary to link together the different specialisms in theory and practice to enable a new approach to literacy to be adopted: one that is based on the developmental needs of each child. *Decoding Dyslexia* is my personal contribution toward achieving this.

Summary

The hypothesis generated by this study suggests that the developmental needs of children, if unmet, can result in problems with literacy which will be reflected through their genetic identities. These are likely to show where they are most *susceptible* and to appear as developmental problems and compensatory learning styles. Signs of 'Type 2' dyslexia become a signal that the child has not integrated fully into the gravitational world and is physically disorientated while 'Type1' shows cognitive incompatibility. Where there are immune-system effects, perhaps highlighted by chromosome 6 involvement, this could act as a warning that some environmental element may be causing difficulties to some children of a particular genetic identity (GI). This understanding gives us the ability to address these elements together with the potential to avoid creating problems for certain individuals. In the future we need to consider everything that may impact upon the developing child's sensory development, and to see dyslexia as the *result* of orientation problems which we can and must address within our cultural as well as educational structures. Children rather than literacy need to become the focus and – paradoxically – by becoming so, literacy will more easily follow.

APPENDIX I

MERGED THEME CODES

The following codes were merged before analysis;

Innate	O
Genetic	G

Both themes became *Genetic* (G)

Learning Style	LS
Dominance Profile	DP

Both themes became *Dominance Profile* (DP)

Major Histocompatibilty Complex	MRC 1
CAT 301 Antibody	CAT 301
Immunological	IMN

Both themes became *Immunological* (IMN)

Visual/middle temporal area	VS/MT
Primary visual area/cortex	PVC/A

Both themes became *Visual/middle temporal area*   (VS/MT)

Lateral geniculate nuclei	(LGN)
Medial geniculate nuclei	(MGN)
Thalamus	(THA)

These three themes became *Thalamus*   (THA)

Balance	
Orientation	(O)

Both themes became *Orientation*

In addition, the single coding of Chromosome (CHR) which fell into only one model, was replaced by specific Chromosome number codings.

THE 126 THEMES

TH	Thought
O	Orientation
T	Talent/Gift
V	Visual Sense
MS	Multisensory
I	Integration
CV	Creativity
DEV	Development
H	Holistic
G	Genetic
CON	Construction
S	Sensory/system
TM	Time
PT	Personality Trait
BR	Brain Region
PH	Phonological/Phonetic
PC	Perception/ual
C	Cure/Corrected
M	Meaning/Concept
IH	Inner-Hearing
SS	Stress/ors/Anxiety
ME	Mind's Eye

I:I	One-to-One
SCAF	Scaffolding/Support
CL	Cross-Lateral
REH	Rehersal
TT	Turn-Taking
PRS	Praise
SL	Slow/ly
TC	Touch Sense
VC	Voicing/Speech Sense
L.RES	Learned Response
SEQ	Sequence
DSEQ	Developmental Sequence
E	Emotion/Affective
VS	Vestibular Sense
PR	Posture
MV	Movement
Ω	Harmony/Conflict
HF	High/Temporal Frequency
LF	Low-Frequency
ACT	Activity
SA	Self-Actualisation
COM	Communication
SC	Self-Conscious/Awareness
SO	Social
U	In-Utero/Fetal
☾/C	Mother/Child Relationship
☾/U	Mother/Unborn Child Relationship
F/C	Father/Child Relationship
RY	Rhythm
☾/VC	Mother's Voice
F/VC	Father's Voice
DD	Developmental Delay

NLD	Non-literary Dyslexia
SEC	Security/Relaxed
☾/F	Parents
☾	Mother
F	Father
SD	Shut-Down
A	Auditory Sense
AC	Auditory Cortex
IND	Individual/Personal
VGN	Vagus Nerve
LED	Left-Ear Dominance
RED	Right-Ear Dominance
BD	Body
EP	Empathy
B	Birth
L.HEM	Left-Hemisphere
R.HEM	Right-Hemisphere
REL	Relationship
LAT	Laterality
L.HND	Left-Handed
R.HND	Right-Handed
DP	Dominance Profile/s
SM	Survival Mechanism
EA	Ear
CB	Cerebellum
CC	Corpus Callosum
CHR1	Chromosome 1
CHR2	Chromosome 2
CHR6	Chromosome 6
CHR15	Chromosome 15
IMN	Immunological
PVA/C	Primary Visual Area/Cortex

LF	Low Frequency
DVP	Dorsal Visual processing
PVS	Parvocellular
SPC	Superior Colliculus
ENV	Environmental Factor/s
PLT	Planum Temporal
A/SYM	A/Symmetry
THA	Thalamus
LTP	Left Temporo-Parietal
CNS	Central Nervous System
♪	Musical
PRX	Primary Reflex
OHC	Optimal Hearing Curve
CN	Cochlear Nucleus
IL	Ipsilateral
PAC	Primary Auditory Cortex
L.EAR	Left Ear
R.EAR	Right Ear
HM	Hormonal
ISA	Intrasylvian Area
STG	Superior Temporal Gyrus
GD	Gender
♂	Male
♀	Female
LS	Limbic System
ANS	Autonomic Nervous System
RAS	Reticular Activating System
BS	Brain Stem
HYP	Hypothalamus
PV	Pre-Verbal
ATNR	Asymmetrical Tonic Neck Reflex
TLR	Tonic Labyrinthine Reflex

STNR	Symmetrical Tonic Neck Reflex
TGR	Tendon Guard Reflex
CIA	Common Integrative Area
PARL	Parietal Lobe
COLL	Superior/Inferior Colliculi

COMMON DENOMINATOR: ORIENTATION (O) DATA FILE

Tomatis Method

Paradigm/Philosophy

> p2, L13: 'It (The ear) provides a sense of special awareness and control of movement and posture through the vestibular system.'

Method

> p9, L26-8: 'The child's spatial orientation is then tested. Tomatis believes that a dyslexic child cannot easily locate him/herself in the universe and this test shows the degree of confusion in localising ability that appears fundamental to them.

JST

Paradigm/Philosophy

P6, L13: 'Binaural pure tone testing can detect confusion or inconsistency in ear advantage-'

Method: None

Bakker's Balance Mode

None

Stein's Magnocellular Theory

Paradigm/Philosophy

> p4, L10: 'One of the most important uses to which visual motion signals are put is to achieve visual perceptual stability.'

Method

p11,L27-28: 'This is aimed at achieving stable binocular dominance and to control visual confusion.'

Helen Irlen SSS

Paradigm/Philosophy

p3,L3: 'Letters such as 'b', 'd' and 'p' can easily be confused.

Method

p12,L29-30: 'By using the technique of spectral modification with coloured lenses, all – not just some – of the distortions will be reduced or eliminated.

Brain Gym

Paradigm/Philosophy

p1, L6: '–a critical place given to the role of movement in learning and of an individual's spatial awareness.

p2, L18: – the integration of information about the body from gravity and motion in space is considered vital in developing an ability to understand and learn.'

Method

p22, L11-15: 'Walk across a narrow bridge, balance beam or tightrope. Swim, ski, skate and surf.

Primary Reflex Inhibition

Paradigm/Philosophy

p1,L.12: 'Posture develops as a child gains control over balance, and balance is dependent upon a mature reflex system.

p2,L26-27: 'This is at the same time when we move from

the horizontal to the vertical world, and it allows us to obtain orientation in a gravity environment.'

Method

p27,Fig 3: ' 90% rotation of the arms and/or loss of balance as a result of head rotation.'

Dore/DDAT

Paradigm/Philosophy

p2,L9: 'Three factors bring about balance;-'

Method

p4,L21-22: 'Posturography (balance strategy) – this includes a) sensory organisation analysis, b) centre of gravity variation and c) adaption response.'

Alpha-to-Omega

Paradigm/Philosophy

p2,L21-23: 'Multisensory methods rely on re-connecting these different senses simultaneously, developing an awareness of the basis or written language and giving control over the child's sensory system.

Method: None.

Music-making

Paradigm/Philosophy

p11,L1-2: 'Music is therefore the first medium of any encounter and the primary orientation system of human beings fro within the womb onwards.

Method

p14,L8: '(piano) can be very difficult for a dyslexic child who is disorientated by trying to read the two visual planes at once.'

Ron Davis Method

Paradigm/Philosophy

> p1,L6: 'Dyselxia is the product of thought and a special way of reacting to the feeling of confusion.'

> p5,L1-4: 'Orientation means knowing where you are in relation to your environment. In-perception, it means finding out the facts and conditions of your surroundings and putting yourself in the proper relation to them.'

Method

> p12,L16: 'Following the assessment comes *Orientation Counselling.*'

Phono-Graphix

Paradigm/Philosophy

> p2,L2: 'The orientation from letter to sound is wrong-'.

> p3,L29-30: 'They become thoroughly confused trying to learn something for which they are developmentally un-ready.'

Method

> p13,L9: '—often lack the left to right orientation needed to distinguish between the sound pictures <d> and <b>.'

Pharmacological methods

Paradigm/Philosophy

> p3,L10-12: 'a cerebellar-vestibular disorder, which makes them prone to feelings of motion sickness.'

Method

> p5,L3-4: '-for whom he prescribed half of one anti-motion sickness drug per day '

Efalex

Paradigm/Philosophy

p2,L23-24: '-anomalies – in the area of the brain involved in coordintion and balance (the cerebellum).

Method: None

RESOURCES FOR
A POSITIVE MANIFESTO FOR DYSLEXIA

Goddard, (2002) *Reflexes, Learning and Behaviour* Fern Ridge, (Contains tests for retained reflexes)

The Institute for Neuro-Physiological Psychology (INPP) Provides Goddard and Blythe's courses for training teachers on incorporating therapeutic exercise programmes into schools. www.inpp.org.uk

Brain Gym exercises for use at home or in school can be found at www.braingym.org

For Gardiner's *Multiple Intelligences* class and teaching materials; *Brain Gym* and *Personalised Teaching* books contact: www.anglo-american.co.uk for a catalogue

BDA website for *Dyslexia friendly Schools* /whole teaching policy is www.bdadyslexia.org.uk

Gurian, M. (2001) *Boys and Girls Learn Differently* (contains practical ideas for gender-specific teaching and some challenging ideas)

Hannaford (1997) *The Dominance Factor* Great Ocean Publishers (contains how to work out 32 dominance profiles and the strengths and weaknesses of each.

Mortimore, T. (2006) *Dyslexia and Learning* Style Whurr Publishers. (Contains further resource section for teaching to individual learning styles.

Reid, G. (2005). *Learning Styles and Inclusion*. Sage.

Winebrenner, S (1996). *Teaching Kids with Learning Difficulties in the Regular Classroom*. Free Spirit Press. (available from anglo-american above)

REFERENCES

Ayers, A. J. (1979/91). *Sensory integration and the child.* Western Psychological Services: Los Angeles, CA.

Berlin, C. J. (1977). Hemispheric asymmetry in auditory tasks. In: *Lateralisation in the nervous system.* Harnad, S., Doty, R., Goldstein, L., Jaynes, J., & G, Krauthamer, (eds). Academic Press: New York.

BDA/DfEE. (1998). *Achieving dyslexia friendly schools: Resource pack.* Reading: British Dyslexia Association.

Berliner, W. (2003) 'A giant leap for dyslexics'. *Guardian,* January 21st.

Birch, H. (1962). Dyslexia and maturation of visual function. In J. Money, (ed). *Reading disability: Progress and research needs in dyslexia.* Baltimore: Johns Hopkins Press.

Bishop, D.V.M. (2004). 'Why I study...Laterality'. *The Psychologist,* (Vol.17), No.9, pp504-505.

Bishop, D., & C. Adams. (1990). A prospective study of the between specific language impairment, phonological disorders and reading retardation. *Journal of Child Psychology and Psychiatry,* (31), pp1027-1050.

Blackemore, S., & U, Frith. (2005). *The learning brain: lessons for education.* Oxford: Blackwell Publishing.

Borchgrevink, H.M. (1982). Prosody and musical rhythm are controlled by the speech Hemisphere. In: M. Clynes, (ed). *Music, Mind and brain – the neuropsychology of music,* pp151-159, New York: Plenum Press.

Bremmer, J.G, (1994). *Infancy (2nd edition).* Blackwell: Oxford.

Broadhurst, C.L., Cunnane, S., & M.A. Crawford. (1998). 'Rift Valley lake fish and shellfish provide brain-specific nutrition for early homo.' *British Journal of Nutrition,* (9), pp3-21.

Bryant, P. (2005). Personal email correspondence. (March 11th 2005).

Bushe-Huey, E. (1913). *The psychology of a pedagogy of reading.*

Calvert, G., Spence, C., and B. Stein. (2004). *The handbook of multisensory processes*. Bradford Books: London.

Cardon, L.R., Smith, S.D., Fulker, D.W., Klimberling, W.J., Pennington, B.F. and Defries, J.C. (1994). Quantitative trait locus for reading disability on Chromosome 6. *Science* 266: 276-278

Choksy, L. (1974). *The Kodaly Method*. Englewood Cliffs, N.J: Prentice-Hall Inc.

Clay, M. (1987). Implementing reading recovery: Systemic adaptions to an educational innovation. *New Zealand Journal of Educational Studies*, 22, pp35-8

CMC, (1998). *The Fourth R*. The Campaign for music in the curriculum: West Horsley, UK.

Cohen Kadosh, R. (2007). 'Study is breakthrough for dyscalculia sufferers'. *Labnews.Co,Uk.* October 2002:
www. shambles.net/pages/learning/sen/dyscalculia/-58k

Combley, M. (2001). *The Hickey Multisensory Language Course* (3rd ed), London: Whurr Publishers Ltd.

Cornelissen, P., Hansen, P.C., Hutton, L., Evangelinou, B., & J.F. Stein. (1997).Magnocellular visual function and children's single word reading. *Vision Research*, (38), pp471-482.

Davis, R. (1997). *The gift of dyslexia*. London: Souvenir Press.

Dennison, P. (1981). *'Switching On': The whole brain answer to dyslexia*. Ventura, CA: Edu-Kinesthetics Inc.

Dennison, P., & G. Dennison. (1985). *Personalised whole brain integration*. Ventura, CA: Edu-Kinesthetics Inc.

DeCasper. A., & W. Fifer. (1980). Of human bonding: newborns prefer their mother's voices. *Science*, (208), pp1174-1176.

Diamond, S., Balvin, R., Diamond, R., (1963). *Inhibition and choice*. Harper Rowe:New York.

Dobson, R. (2000). 'Could a travel sickness pill beat dyslexia?' *Daily Mail*, June 6th.

DORE (2001). *Promotional video*.

Douglas, S., & P. Willatts. (1994). The relationship between musical ability and literacy skills. *Journal of research in reading*, 17(2), pp99-107.

Douglas, S., & R.S. Johnston. (1995). The relationship between musical ability and literacy skills. *SERA*. (*95*). pp85-89.

EKF, (2003). Research Study Summaries: A chronology of annotated research study summaries in the field of educational kinesiology. *Brain Gym International*. Ventura, USA: The Educational Kinesiology Foundation.

Evans, J.R., & N, Park. (1995). Quantitative EEG abnormalities in a sample of dyslexic persons. *Journal of Neurotherapy*: www.snr-jnt.org/journalnt/jnt (2-1)1.html

Fernald, G.M. (1943). *Remedial techniques in basic school subjects*. New York: McGraw-Hill.

Fagerheim, T. et.al (1999). A new gene (DYX3) for dyslexia is located on Chromosome 2. *Journal of Medical Genetics* 36: 664-669.

Fawcett, A. 2002: A framework for understanding dyslexia. DFES website: Http//www.dfes.gov.uk/readwriteplus/understandingdyslexia

Field, T., Woodson, R., Greenberg., & D. Cohen. (1982). Discrimination and imitation of facial expressions by neonates. *Science*. (218), p179-181.

Fletcher, J., Shaywitz, S., Shankweiler, D., Katz, L., et.al. (1994). Cognitive profiles of reading disability: comparisons of discrepancy and low achievement definitions. *Journal of Educational Psychology,* 86 (1), 6-23.

Freeman,C.K. (2000). A summary of a Brain Gym research project on reading. *Brain Gym Journal,* December, pp2-3.

Galaburda, A.M., & M. Livingstone. (1993). Evidence for a magnocellular defect in developmental dyslexia, pp65-73. In: P. Tallal., A.M. Galaburda, R.R. Llinas., and C,von Euler, (eds). Temporal information processing in the nervous system. *Annals of the New York Academy of Science*, (682), pp70-82.

Galaburda, A. M., Menard, M.T., & G.D. Rosen. (1994). Evidence for aberrant auditory anatomy in developmental dyslexia. *Proceedings of the National Academy of Science USA* (913), pp8010-8013.

Gardiner, H. (1983). *Frames of Mind: The theory of multiple intelligence*. New York: Basic Books.

Gillingham, A. and Stillman, B. 1946/1969: Remedial training for children with specific disabilities in reading, spelling and penmanship. Cambridge, Mass Educators Publishing Service.

Goddard, S. (2002). *Reflexes, learning and behaviour: A window into the child's Mind*. Oregon: Fern Ridge Press.

Goddard, S. (2005). Releasing educational potential through movement: A summary of individual studies carried out using the INPP test battery and developmental exercise programme for use in schools with children with special needs. *Child Care in Practice,* Vol.11, 4, 415-432.

Goddard, S, (2006). Cerebellar theory should not be discounted in response to aggressive marketing strategy. *The dyslexia online journal*@inpp.org.uk

Gopnik, A., Meltzoff, A., & P. Kuhl. (2005). *How babies think: The science of childhood.* London: Weidenfeld and Nicolson.

Goswami, U. (2003). How to beat dyslexia. *The Psychologist,* (16) No.9, pp462-465.

Goswami,U. (2004). Neuroscience and education. *British Journal of Educational Psychology,* (74), pp1-14, BPS Press.

Goswami, U., Thomson, J., Richardson, U., Stainthorpe, R., Hughes, D., & S, Rosen. (2002). Amplitude envelope onsets and developmental dyslexia: A new hypothesis. *Proceedings of the National Academy of Sciences,* 99 (16), pp10911-10916.

Grigorenko, E.L., Wood, F.B., Meyer, M.S., Hart, L.A., Speed, W.C., Shuster, A. and Pauls, D. L. (1997). Susceptibility loci for distinct components of developmental dyslexia on Chromosomes 6 & 15. *American Journal of Human Genetics,* 60, 27-39.

Gurian, M. (2001). *Boys and girls learn differently.* Jossey-Bass: San Francisco.

Hairston, D., Burdette., J.H., Flowers, D., Wood, F.B., & M. Wallace. (2005). *Altered temporal profile of visual-auditory multisensory interactions in dyslexia.* In press.

Hallam, S. (2002). The effects of music on studying and behaviour. *British Psychological Society Education Section,* pp18 -19.

Hanley, (1997). Reading and spelling impairments in undergraduate students with developmental dyslexia. Journal of research in reading (Special issue: Dyslexia in literate adults). 20 (1): 22-23.

Hannaford, C. (1995). *Smart moves: Why learning is not all in your head.* Arlington, Virginia: Great Ocean Publishing.

Hannaford, C. (1997). *The Dominance Factor: How knowing your dominant eye, ear, brain, hand & foot can improve your learning.* Arlington, Virginia: Great Ocean Publishing.

Hart, B., & T.R. Risley. (1995). *Meaningful differences.* Baltimore, Md : Brooks.

Hatcher, P.J., Hulme, C. and Ellis, A.W. (1994). Ameliorating early reading failure by integrating teaching of reading and phonological skills. The phonological linkage hypothesis. *Child Development*, 65, 41-57.

Hepper, P. (2005). Unravelling our beginnings. *The Psychologist*, August, (Vol.18), No. 8, pp474-477.

Hodges, D. (1996). Neuromusical Research: A review of the literature. In: Hodges, D. *Handbook of music psychology, (2nd edition)*. San Antonia: IMR Press.

Hornsby, B. (1984). *Overcoming dyslexia*. London: Martin Dunitz.

Hornsby, B. and Shear. F. 1975: Alpha to Omega. London: Heinemann Educational Books.

Horrobin, D.F., & C.N. Bennett. (1999). 'New gene targets related to schizophrenia and other psychiatric disorders: enzymes, binding proteins and transport proteins involved in phospholipid and fatty acid metabolism'. *Prostaglandines, leukotriens and Essential Fatty Acids,* 60, (3), p141-167.

Horwood, J., & D. Fergusson. (1998). Breast feeding and later cognitive and academic outcomes. *Pediatrics*, (101), pp1-7.

Hulme, C., & M.J. Snowling. (1997). *Dyslexia: Biology, cognition and interventions*. London: Whurr.

Irlen, H. (1991). *Reading by the colours*. New York: Avery Publishing Group Inc Jacques-Dalcroze, E. (1930). Eurythmics: Art and Education. London: Chatto and Windus.

Jensen, J.H., et.al. (1989). Unilateral sensori-aural hearing loss in children: Cognitive abilities with respect to right/left ear differences. *British Journal of Audiology*, (23), pp215-220.

Johansen, K. (1988). *Reading and re-creation*. Paper presented at UKRA conference, (July), University of Leicester. Bornholm: Dyslexia Research Lab.

Johansen, K. (1991). *Diagnosing dyslexia: The screening of auditory laterality*. Bornholm: Dyslexia Research Lab.

Johansen, K. (1994). General laterality, unilateral hearing loss, ear advantage and language problems. Chester: *INFF monograph series*.

Kappers, E.J., & H.L. Hamburger. (1994). Neuropsychological treatment of dyslexia in outpatients. In: Light, R., & G.Spyer, (eds). (1994). *The Balance Model of Dyslexia*. Van Gorcum: Assen & Company.

Karpt, A. (2001). It's a pity reading pleasure can't be tested. *Guardian,*

Dec.6th.

Klaus, M.H., Kennell, J.H., & P. H. Klaus. (1995). *Bonding.* London: Cedar.

Klingberg, T., Hedehus. M., Temple, E., Salz, T., Gabrieli, J., Moseley, M., & R. Poldrack. (2000). Microstructure of temporo-parietal white matter as a basis for reading ability: Evidence from diffusion tensor magnetic resonance imaging. *Neuron,* (Vol.25). pp493-500.Kolb, B., & I.Wishaw. (1996). *Fundamentals of human neuropsychology,* (4th edition). New York: W.H. Freeman and Company.

Larsen, S. (1989). Laesning og cerebral integration: Et bidrag til kvalifikation-sudviklingens psykologi. *Disputats. Koebenhavn:* Gyldendal Levinson, H.N. (1980). *A solution to the riddle of dyslexia.* New York: Springer Veriag.

Levinson, H.N. (1988). *The Cerebellar-Vestibular basis of learning disabilities in children, adolescents and adults: Hypothesis and study.* In: Perceptual & Motor Skills, (Vol. 67).

Levinson, H.L. (1991). *The upside down kids.* New York: M. Evans.

Livingstone, M.S., Rosen, G.D., Drislane, F.W., & A.M, Galaburda, A.M. (1991). Physiological and anatomical evidence for a magnocellular defect in developmental dyslexia. *Proceedings of the National Academy of Science,* USA, (88), pp7943-7947.

Long, M. (2000). *The psychology of education.* Routledge Falmer: London

Lorusso, M.L. (1994). A critical review of Bakker's balance model of dyslexia. In: Light, R. & G.Spyer, (eds). (1994). *The Balance Model of dyslexia.* Van Gorcum: Assen & Company.

Lucas, A., Morley, R., & T. Cole, et al. (1992). 'Breast milk and subsequent intelligence quotient in children born pre-term.' *Lancet* (339), pp261-264.

Macdonnell, L.E.F., Skinner, F. K., Ward, P. E., Glen, A. I.M., Glen, A.C.A.,

Macdonald, D. J., Boyle, R. M. & D.E. Horrobin. (2000). In: Stein, J. (2001). The magnocellular theory of developmental dyslexia. *Dyslexia,* (7), pp12-36.

Maclean, M., Bryant, P.E., & L, Bradley, (1987). Rhymes, nursery rhymes and reading in early childhood. *Merrill-Palmer Quarterly,* **33**, pp255-281.

Macrae, (1998). *The Early Years: Despatches Report.* Channel 4 Television

Mallick, S. (2003). *Frontiers,* Oct. 26, BBC Radio 4.

Mortimore, M. (2006). *Dyslexia and learning style: A practitioner's handbook.*

Whurr: London.

McGuinness, D. (1998). *Why children can't read: And what we can do about it.* London: Penguin.

McGuinness. C., & G, McGuinness. (1998). *Reading Reflex: The foolproof Phono-Graphix method for teaching your child to read.* London: Penguin.

McPhillips, M. (2001). The role of persistent primary-reflexes in reading delay. *Dyslexia Review*, (Vol.13). No.1, Autumn, pp4-7.

McPhillips, M., Hepper, P., & G. Mulhern. (2000). Effects of replicating primary reflex movements on specific reading difficulties in children: A randomised, double blind, controlled trial. *The Lancet.* (Vol. 355). February 12, pp535-451.

Merzenich, M.M. (1993). Neural mechanisms underlying temporal integration, segmentation and input sequence representation: Some implications for the origin of learning disabilities. In: In: Tallal, P., Galaburda, A.M., Von Euler, C., & R.Linus, (eds). *Temporal information processing in the nervous system.* New York: The New York Academy of Sciences.

Miles, E. 1989: The Bangor Dyslexia Teaching System. London: Whurr.

Miles, T. R. and Miles. E. 1990: Dyslexia: A hundred years on. Milton Keynes: Open University Press.

Morton, J. 2004: Understanding developmental disorders: A causal modelling approach. Oxford: Blackwell.

Mutter, V. (2003). *Early reading development and dyslexia.* London: Whurr.

Newman, J. (1995). How breast milk protects newborns. *Scientific American*, December, pp58-61.

Nicolson, R. (2005) Dyslexia: Beyond The Myth. *The Psychologist.* Vol.18 No 11. 658-659.

Nicolson, R., & A.J. Fawcett. (1996/2004). *The Dyslexia Early Screening Test.* London: The Psychological Corporation.

Nicolson, R., & A. J. Fawcett. (1999). Developmental dyslexia: The role of the cerebellum. *Dyslexia*, (5): pp155-177.

Nicolson, R., and D. Reynolds. (2003). Science, sense and synergy: response to commentators. *Dyslexia,* 9: 167-176.

Olson, R.K., Kliegel, R. and Davidson, B.L. (1985). Individual and developmental differences in reading disability. In G.E. MacKinnon and T.G. Waller (Editors). *Reading Research: Advances in Theory and*

Practice, Vol. 4, New York: Academic Press, 1-64.

Olson, R.K. 2004: SSR, Environment and genes. *Scientific studies of reading,* (8) 2, 111-124.

Oyler, R.F., Oyler, A.L., & N. D. Matkin. (1987). Warning: a unilateral hearing loss may be detrimental to a child's academic career. In: *The Hearing Journal.* pp18-22.

Pennington, B. 2002: *The development of psychopathology*: Nature and nurture. London: The Guilford Press.

Pidgeon, N. 1996: Grounded Theory: Theoretical background. In: Richardson, J.T.E. (editor): *Handbook of qualitative research methods.* Leicester (UK): BPS.

Pert, C. (1997). *Molecules of emotion.* London: Simon & Schuster Ltd.

Pinel, J. P. (1990). *Biopsychology.* Needham Heights, MA: Allyn & Bacon.

Poole, J.E. (2005) *Towards an ecological theory of developmental dyslexia.* Unpublished PhD. Exeter University.

Pumfrey, D., & R, Reason. (1991). *Specific learning difficulties, (Dyslexia): Challenges and responses.* Windsor: NFER-Nelson.

Ramsay, D.S. (1984). Onset of duplicated syllable babbling and unimanual handedness in infants: evidence for developmental change in hemispheric specialisation? *Developmental Psychology*, 20, 64-71

Reason, R. (2001). Educational practice and dyslexia' *Psychologist,* 14, pp298-301.

Reid, G. (2005). *Learning styles and inclusion.* Paul Chapman Publishing: London.

Resnick, L. (1987). Learning in school and out. *The Educational Researcher* (US), December, p18.

Reynolds, D., Nicolson, R.I. and Hambly H. (2003). Evaluation of an exercise-based treatment for children with reading difficulties. *Dyslexia* 9, 48-71.

Richardson, A.J., McDaid, A.M., Calvin, D.M. et.al. (2000). Reduced behavioural and learning problems in children with specific learning difficulties after supplementation with highly unsaturated fatty acids: a randomised double-blind placebo-controlled trial. *Federation of European neuroscience societies.* (FENS 000). Brighton.

Robertson, P. (1998). Presenting the case for music. *Yes,* (28), Spring, pp19-21.

Sanger, S., & J. Kelly. (1995). *The magic square.* New York: Bantam.

Savan, A. (2002). In. Hallam, S. The effects of music on studying and behaviour. *British Psychological Society Education Section.* pp.18-19.

Selikowitz, M. (1998). *Dyslexia: The facts.* (2nd edition). Oxford: OUP.

Schrager, O. L. (2001). Posture and balance: important markers for the children's learning development. Paper presented at *Symposium,* Atlanta, Georgia.

Smyth, A. (2001). On reading, reflex and research. *The Psychologist,* (Vol.14) No.2, February, pp81-83.

Snowling, M. (2000). *Dyslexia.* (2nd Edition) Oxford: Blackwell.

Springer, S., & G.Deutsch. (1991). *Left brain, right brain: Perspectives from cognitive neuroscience.* New York: W.H. Freeman & Co.

Stanovich, K. (1993) Introduction. In D.M. Willows, R.S. Kruk and E. Corcos (Editors). *Visual processes in reading and reading disabilities.* New Jersey: Lawrence Erlbaum Associates.

Stanovich, K. (1994). Annotations: does dyslexia exist? *Journal of Child Psychology and Psychiatry,* 35 (4), 579-595

Stein, J. (2000). Outcome of treatment of visual problems in children with reading difficulties. *PATOSS Bulletin,* pp9-14.

Stein, J. F. (2001). The magnocellular theory of developmental dyslexia. *Dyslexia,* (7): pp12-36.

Stein, J.F., Riddell, P. and Fowler, M.S. (1988). Disordered vergence eye movement control in dyslexic children. *British journal of opthalmology,* 72, 162-166.

Stein, J.F., & V. Walsh. (1997). To see but not to read: The magnocellular theory of dyslexia. *Trends in neuroscience,* (20), pp147-152.

Steiner, R. (1981). *A modern art of education.* London: Rudolph Steiner Press.

Sternberg, R.J. (1997). *Thinking styles.* Cambridge: Cambridge University Press.

Stordy, J., & M. Nicholl. (2002). *The LCP Solution.* Oxford: Macmillan.

Tallal, P. 2004: Improving language and literacy is a matter of time. *Nature Reviews* 5, September, 1-7.

Taylor, K. E., Higgins, C. H., Calvin, C.M., Hall, J.A., Easton, T., McDaid, A.M., & A.J. Richardson. (2000). In: Stein, J. (2001). The magnocellular theory of developmental dyslexia. *Dyslexia,*(7), pp12-36.

TEDS. (2006) Kings College London College Archives: http//www.aim25.ac.uk

Thomson, J, B. (1994). *Natural Childhood.* London: Gaia Books.

Tomatis, A. (1957/1991). *The conscious ear: My life of transformation through listening.* New York: Station Hill Press.

Tomatis, A. (1972). *Education and dyslexia.* Switzerland: AIAPP.

Trevarthan, C. (2003). *Frontiers,* Oct. 26. BBC Radio 4.

Vellutino, F.R. (1979). *Dyselxia: theory and research.* Cambridge, Massachusetts: The MIT Press.

Viadero, D. (1999). *Irlen lenses: A cure for reading ills?* Irlen Centre website: www.irlencentralengland.co.uk

Vincent, A., Deacon, R., Blamire, A.,W. Pendlebury, S., et.al (2000). Behavioural and cerebellar MRS findings in mice exposed in utero to serum from mothers of children with neurodevelopmental disorders. *Proceedings of the international society of magnetic resonance medicine,* 1080.

Wilsher, C. R. (1996). Pharmacological treatment of dyslexia. In: Vanden Bos, K., Siegel, L.S., Bakker, D.J., & D.L. Share, (eds). *Current directions in dyslexia research.* B.V, Lisse: Swets & Zeitlinger.

Winebrenner, S. (1996). *Teaching kids with learning difficulties in the regular classroom.* Free Spirit: Minneapolis

Wisby, A. (1980). *Learning through music.* Lancaster: MIT.Press.

Zaichkowsky, L.D., Zaichkowsky, L.B. and T.J. Martinek. (1980). *The child and physical activity.* St Louis: Mosby.

Printed in the United Kingdom by
Lightning Source UK Ltd., Milton Keynes
142306UK00001B/13/P